A TOUR OF DUTY

DOUGLAS KAMMEN AND SIDDHARTH CHANDRA

A TOUR OF DUTY:
CHANGING PATTERNS OF MILITARY POLITICS
IN INDONESIA IN THE 1990S

EQUINOX
PUBLISHING
JAKARTA KUALA LUMPUR

Equinox Publishing (Asia) Pte Ltd
No 3. Shenton Way
#10-05 Shenton House
Singapore 068805

www.EquinoxPublishing.com

A Tour of Duty:
Changing Patterns of Military Politics in Indonesia in the 1990s
by Douglas Kammen and Siddharth Chandra

ISBN 978-602-8397-13-1

First Equinox Edition 2010

Printed in the United States

1 3 5 7 9 10 8 6 4 2

Table of Contents

INTRODUCTION

On October 1, 1965, in response to an attempted coup by low-ranking officers, Major General Soeharto seized command of the Indonesian military. Having quashed the attempted coup and squarely pinned blame for the coup and the murders of senior generals on the Indonesian Communist Party, Soeharto and the Army proceeded to conduct and direct a massacre of horrifying proportions. In March 1966, Soeharto forced then-President Sukarno to relinquish executive authority. Two years later Soeharto had himself appointed President of Indonesia. On May 21, 1998, thirty-two years after coming to power, General Soeharto was forced to resign in the face of nation-wide outrage, protests, and riots against his corrupt and authoritarian rule.

Over a span of three decades the Soeharto regime distinguished itself from many other authoritarian states. Retired from active military service in 1976, Soeharto was only rarely referred to as a general, preferring the internationally approved title of President.[1] National parliamentary elections were held every five years, though carefully orchestrated to ensure that the ruling party, Golkar, won by a comfortable margin. During this time, the Indonesian military transformed itself from a poorly trained force characterized by its origins in guerrilla warfare into a modern standing military. The Army successfully passed leadership from the *Angkatan 1945* (Generation of 1945), which fought in the revolution against Dutch colonial rule, to a younger generation of academy-trained officers.

During the past three decades, the military in general and the Army in particular have played a central role in Indonesian politics.

---

1   One notable recent exception occurred on October 5, 1997, Indonesian Armed Forces Day, when Soeharto wore a military uniform and was promoted to five-star general.

Despite the omission of military honorifics preceding Soeharto's name and the facade of democratic institutions, the Army remains the single strongest institution in the country. One fifth of all legislative seats are reserved for members of the military.[2] Military personnel are commonly appointed to serve as district administrative heads and provincial governors. Senior military officers are also appointed as ministers and to key posts within the ministries, though this has decreased during the 1990s. The military routinely intervenes in all aspects of civilian life, ranging from elections to the operations of mass and non-governmental organizations, and from the press to university affairs. It has done so, despite an insistence on the "rule of law," often in violation of the Indonesian legal code.

Despite its general adherence to international military norms and overall organizational strength, it would be wrong to assume that the Indonesian military is a perfectly oiled machine. Just as the military has overcome numerous institutional and political problems (through the use of finesse as well as force), new conflicts and contradictions have emerged. Two of these pose the particular puzzles with which this work is most immediately concerned. First, given the military's dominance of the political system, why did large-scale personnel reshuffles in the Army take place more and more rapidly during the 1990s? Taken at face value, there is no apparent reason why this should happen within a modern standing army. Second, if during the 1990s Soeharto came to rely on the appointment of relatives and officers who had served him in a personal capacity to retain his control over the military, why then did the military not defend the embattled dictator in May 1998? In this work we will argue that the answers to these questions are not to be found in Jakarta politics in the 1990s, but rather in decisions made in the 1960s regarding the structure of the Army officer corps and centered on the National Military Academy in Magelang, Central Java.

---

2 This applies to the People's Representative Council (DPR), as well as the provincial and district legislatures (DPRD I and II). As will be discussed, in 1995 the number of seats reserved for the military in the DPR was reduced to 15 percent.

THE INDONESIAN ARMY IN THE 1990s

We can begin to paint a picture of Indonesian military politics in the 1990s by introducing five points of conflict which fundamentally shape its current condition. Some of these issues are purely organizational, others concern the relationship between the military and the Indonesian political system, and still others stem from changing civil-military relations.

The first problem involves generational transitions: during the 1990s there has been persistent dissatisfied murmuring from senior and retired officers about the military and its position in national politics. Generational divides, of course, are not new in the Indonesian military. By the early 1980s the *Angkatan 1945* generation that had fought in the Indonesian revolution against the Dutch had retired, passing leadership to a post-war generation of officers. In the late 1980s a second transfer occurred, with this latter generation, in turn, passing leadership to officers who had graduated from Nasution's National Military Academy during the early 1960s. These generational shifts were accompanied by grumbling among senior and retired officers about the inexperience and lack of political commitment of their juniors. Upset at having been passed over for senior posts or forcibly retired to make way for academy-trained officers, this older generation was disparagingly referred to as the "sick-at-heart brigade" (*barisan sakit hati*).

A second conflict within the Indonesian military involved tensions between members of the military elite and Soeharto. Although not new, this issue arose once again during the late 1980s and continued to haunt Indonesian politics throughout the 1990s. Members of the Armed Forces elite commonly portrayed the problem in terms of maintaining military professionalism and autonomy. This, of course, necessitates limiting (if not entirely preventing) presidential meddling in the appointment process. For Soeharto, however, the appointment of relatives and officers with whom he had worked closely was thought by many observers to be an important means of maintaining control over the military and, by extension, over what had become an increasingly unwieldy political system.

Together, the question of generational change and tensions between the military and the President brings us to a third point: this involves the discussions (and posturing) during the preparations for the 1997 national legislative election and 1998 session of the People's Consultative Assembly (MPR) to select the President for the next five-year term. For the military as a whole, the run-up to the 1997 election was an opportunity to flex its muscles and display to a restive populace its organizational might along with the hardware to back it up.[3] Within the officer corps, there was also genuine concern about the excesses of the Soeharto regime and its failure to develop a more open and democratic political system. Others viewed the election period as an opportunity to participate in ongoing maneuvering with their eyes on the post-Soeharto future.

Most observers agreed that the question of political succession hinged in the first instance on the selection of the vice-president for the 1998-2003 term, particularly given Soeharto's advanced age and the recurrent reports about his ill health. This was an issue with thorny precedents. Several months prior to the 1993 session of the MPR, members of the Armed Forces faction of parliament pre-empted the President by nominating General Try Sutrisno for vice-president before Soeharto had an opportunity to make his own wishes known. Soeharto was furious, but was forced to accept the Army's decision. While the Armed Forces clearly expected that the vice-president selected in 1998 would be a military man, the President remained intent on retaining his own prerogative and made it clear that he would not take kindly to the sort of embarrassment created in 1993. In this Soeharto was successful, and Minister of Technology B. J. Habibie was unanimously selected to the vice-presidency. As events would have it, the question of political succession was answered sooner than most observers imagined: a mere two months after the general session of the MPR, Soeharto was forced to resign, and a German-trained aeronautical engineer with outlandish economic ideas and little support acceded to the presidency.

Recent political developments in Indonesia are not limited to those instigated by the elite, of course. This brings us to a fourth point: the past several years have seen a marked rise not only in open protest,

---

3 What is remarkable is not simply the preparations, elaborate as they were, but the accompanying public show of force. The media regularly reported on training exercises carried out by these election security troops. Photographs show rows of M16s arranged in elegant tripods; lines of tanks and armored vehicles draped in barbed wire; official inspections of spit-'n-polished infantry battalions, complete with M16s; and"anti-riot" troops demonstrating their proficiency with wooden clubs and rattan shields.

but in outbursts of mass violence as well. This was so pronounced that in 1996 the National Police issued statistics explaining that incidents of mass violence were up 80 percent over the previous year.[4] This was to be a mere prelude. During 1997 and early 1998, the collapse of the Indonesian rupiah, the severity of the ensuing economic crisis, and the sharp rise in the prices of basic commodities (including rice, cooking oil, and petroleum) fueled further, and more serious, outbreaks of violence throughout the country. While members of the Armed Forces have long viewed sporadic disturbances as justification for continued military involvement in all spheres of civilian life, massive demonstrations and widespread violence tested the unity and resolve of the military in new ways. As events would have it, the military remained united (though it was necessary to remove several problematic officers from their posts) and, with several tragic exceptions, refrained from a bloody crackdown on hungry and angry civilians.

A fifth and final point, or more precisely cluster of points, has to do with changing civil-military relations. During the 1980s it was commonplace for officers to be rewarded for the use of force and outright repression as responses against national threats. Commanding officers and the troops involved were routinely praised for preventing "subversion" and the latent dangers of "communism," for preventing the occurrence of "*peristiwa*" (incidents), and for maintaining "order and security." These officers were frequently honored with medals, promoted in rank, and appointed to prestigious posts. During the past several years, however, Army officers have no longer been rewarded for the use of violence against civilians. We have seen instead a growing tendency for the military to punish personnel who act outside of the chain of command, use excessive force, or violate legal or human rights. In this respect, the handling of the November 12, 1991 massacre at the Santa Cruz cemetery in Dili, East Timor, marks a turning-point in military practice. Since then the military has made a show of punishing officers elsewhere under whose command violence is committed against civilians.[5]

---

4   See "Peristiwa kekerasan masal meningkat 80 persen, " *Angkatan Bersenjata*, January 25, 1997.

5   Instances of this include officers involved in the handling of protests during the 1994 meeting of the Asia Pacific Economic Cooperation forum; the 1996 riots in Ngabang, West Kalimantan; the 1993 Nipah affair in Madura; and the 1996 riots in Tasikmalaya, West Java.

Disciplinary measures have not been limited to the officer corps. A parallel, if not stronger, campaign has been waged against non-commissioned military personnel who violate regulations.[6] Gambling, the sale of drugs, extortion, and the beating and torture of civilians have all resulted in stern disciplinary measures. This is not to suggest that the Indonesian military has ended the use of strong-arm tactics; nor have these disciplinary campaigns much revised the popular perception of military personnel as corrupt, brutal, and above the law. The significance of these measures, rather, lies in their effect on morale within the military itself. Heightened discipline, the punishment of officers for misconduct, and the scapegoating of officers only make the officer corps all the more cautious.

As the Army has discouraged the use of violence by local commanders against civilians, it has encouraged the National Police, which in Indonesia is a branch of the Armed Forces, to play a more prominent role in maintaining internal security. Members of the military elite have made repeated statements about the need for the police to take primary responsibility in matters of internal security, in particular the handling of demonstrations, strikes, and riots.[7] It was recently announced that the size of the national police force will be increased from the current 180, 000 to 192, 000 personnel.[8] The elite Mobile Brigade (*Brimob*) has been involved in a number of high-profile cases, including the July 27, 1996 attack on the headquarters of the Indonesian Democratic Party (PDI) in Jakarta, the May 1997 riots in Banjarmasin, and the handling of the May 1997 campaign violence in Madura. There has even been renewed discussion about providing the police with greater autonomy by separating the police from the Armed Forces.[9]

---

6 For recent statements, see "Dan Puspom ABRI kepada polisi: Tegur dan kalau perlu tangkap prajurit yang melanggar, " *Angkatan Bersenjata*, September 29, 1997.

7 See the feature series "Langkah-langkah Baru Mengedepankan Polisi, " *Forum Keadilan*, April 7, 1997, pp. 100-108.

8 See "Buku Putih Hankam RI '97: Personil dan material ABRI akan ditambah, " *Angkatan Bersenjata*, July 23, 1997. In June 1997, Lieutenant General Soeyono, then Chief of the General Staff of the Armed Forces, explained that the current ratio of one police officer for every 1, 200 Indonesian citizens needed to be increased to one police officer for every five hundred citizens. See "Pemekaran Satuan Elit Bukan untuk Hadapi Gangguan Pemilu, " *Bernas*, June 29, 1997.

9 See, for example, the conflicting views expressed in "Membangun Polisi yang Dipercaya Masyarakat, " *Forum Keadilan*, July 15, 1996, pp. 100-102. For a more recent discussion, see "Merindukan Polisi yang Mandiri, " *Forum Keadilan*, July 13, 1998, pp. 82-86.

This monograph seeks to provide a coherent framework within which to understand these changes in the military, as well as to inform analysis of the position of the military in the post-Soeharto era.

RECENT EXPLANATIONS

There is now an extensive and varied literature on the Indonesian Armed Forces (Angkatan Bersenjata Republik Indonesia; ABRI). A number of authors, both Indonesian and foreign, have written historical works on the origins, development, and transformation of the Indonesian Army from a guerrilla force to a modern (and some would say professional) institution under the Soeharto regime.[10] Studies of the attempted coup in 1965 have addressed conflicts inside the Armed Forces and the origins of military rule in Indonesia.[11] Other scholars have focused on the military elite during the early years of the New Order.[12] We will be interested in investigating significant trends in officer career advancement and length of job tenure that these more traditional analyses of the Indonesia military, focused on ideological and political factors, have tended to disregard.

Over the past decade and a half there has been a veritable outpouring of works about the ideology of the Indonesian military. The best of these offer considered analyses of the tensions between Javanese and western military traditions, and the ways that these tensions have shaped the political role of the Armed Forces and civil-military relations.[13] Others have approached the question of the Indonesian military's dual function through theoretical consideration of the new military professionalism.[14]

---

10 Ruth McVey, "The Post-Revolutionary Transformation of the Indonesian Army," Part I, *Indonesia* 11 (April 1971): 131-175, and Part II, *Indonesia* 13 (April 1972): 147-182; Ulf Sundhaussen, *The Road to Power* (Kuala Lumpur: Oxford University Press, 1982); and Robert Lowry, *The Armed Forces of Indonesia* (St. Leonards, NSW: Allen & Unwin, 1996).

11 These include Benedict Anderson and Ruth McVey, *A Preliminary Analysis of the October 1, 1965 Coup in Indonesia* (Ithaca, NY: Cornell Modern Indonesia Project, 1971); Harold Crouch, *The Army and Politics in Indonesia* (Ithaca, NY: Cornell University Press, 1988); and the official army version, Nugroho Notosusanto and Ismail Saleh, *The Coup Attempt of the 'September 30th Movement' in Indonesia* (Jakarta: Penbimbing Masa, 1988).

12 Of these, perhaps the best is David Jenkins, *Suharto and his Generals: Indonesian Military Politics 1975-1983* (Ithaca, NY: Cornell Modern Indonesia Project, 1984).

13 Peter Britton, "Military Professionalism in Indonesia: Javanese and Western Military Traditions" (PhD dissertation, Monash University, 1982).

14 See, for example, Ian MacFarling, *The Dual Function of the Indonesian Armed Forces: Military Politics in Indonesia* (Sydney: Australian Defence Studies Centre, The University of New South

The reasons for this emphasis on ideology are twofold. On the one hand, the longevity of the Soeharto regime led scholars to seek reasons why officers and civilians alike accepted the military's dominant place in socio-political affairs. On the other hand, and of perhaps greater importance, scholars have devoted attention to military ideology because it is readily accessible and does not require painstakingly detailed attention to the appointment and promotional process within the officer corps.

The most serious and sustained attempt to interpret the internal dynamics of the Indonesian military has been made by the editors of the journal *Indonesia* in an ongoing series of articles. Over the past decade, these essays have highlighted "conflicts between President Soeharto and many senior officers which started to be visible in early 1988."[15] The extensive personnel transfers that took place within the military elite during July and August 1993 were explained as "palace-inspired countermeasures and/or supplementary rectifications." The editors write:

> The broader context for these maneuverings is without any doubt the political struggle between President Suharto and the Army which has been openly manifest since at least February 27, 1988, when the President abruptly dismissed Murdani as Commander of the Armed Forces, just before the March session of the MPR; and was exacerbated by the crisis over the Dili Massacre of November 12, 1991, the contest for control of Golkar, and the naming of a new Vice President in the spring of [1993].[16]

This same line of argument has been maintained and deepened in subsequent issues. In the October 1994 update, the editors explain that "[a]s a result of the long-simmering conflicts between the President and senior officers and Soeharto's adroit politicking, the army is now

---

Wales, 1996) and Bilveer Singh, *The Dual Function of the Indonesian Armed Forces: Origins, Actualization, and Implementations for Stability and Development* (Singapore: Singapore Institute of International Affairs, 1995).

15 The Editors, "Current Data on the Indonesian Military Elite: January 1, 1992 - August 31, 1993, " *Indonesia* 56 (October 1993): 119.

16 Ibid., p. 123.

deeply divided."[17] Here the editors highlight the difference in perspective between senior military officers attempting to maintain what they call "institutional rationality" in the face of Presidential caprice, and the President and palace's concern about the extent to which the officer corps is "contaminated" by association with retired General Benny Moerdani, the former Commander-in-Chief of the Armed Forces. A year later, analysis of the continuing rotations of officers remained virtually unchanged:

> The reshuffles were aimed at easing out Benny Murdani's men, to serve as palace countermeasures against Gen. Edi Sudradjat's strategic appointments in his brief glory days to safeguard 'army institutional rationality, and more recently to ease out officers whom Wismoyo Arismunandar protected...[18]

There can be no doubt that Soeharto was concerned about the continuing influence that Moerdani held over the officer corps. Likewise, there is ample evidence of Soeharto's ongoing efforts to maintain control over the military through appointment to strategic senior posts of relatives and officers who had previously served him personally. But as this monograph will argue, the same analysis may be inadequate for understanding the increasingly rapid and intensive waves of rotations throughout the Army during the 1990s.

A second line of analysis has highlighted relations between ABRI and Islam and its leaders. Tensions between ABRI and Islam date back to the revolution and the regional rebellions of the 1950s. At the time of the February-March 1995 personnel changes, Harold Crouch argued in an interview that the tandem of ABRI Commander-in-Chief Feisal Tanjung and newly installed Army Chief of Staff General Hartono represented a significant move towards more cordial military-Islamic relations.[19] Generals Feisal and Hartono, in close collaboration with Siti Hardijanti Rukmana, President Soeharto's daughter, did indeed make highly visible

---

17 The Editors, "Current Data on the Indonesian Military Elite: September 1, 1993 - August 31, 1994, " *Indonesia* 58 (October 1994).

18 The Editors, "Current Data on the Indonesian Military Elite: September 1, 1993 - September 30, 1995, " *Indonesia* 60 (October 1995): 104.

19 Interview with Harold Crouch in 'ABRI dan Islam, " *Tiras*, February 23, 1995.

overtures to Islam through visits to *pesantrén* (rural Islamic schools), contributions to mosques, and the release of a number of Islamic political prisoners.[20] This line of argument was repeated by one of the contributors to a report by the Indonesian Academy of Sciences (Lembaga Ilmu Pengetahuan Indonesia; LIPI). The author writes:

> ...the improvement of relations between the government and Islam has been marked, among other things, by elements within ABRI approaching the *pesantrén*...This demonstrates clearly that there has been an important change in ABRI-Islamic relations...[21]

But however important their positions, the appointment of several new officers to head an institution as large as the Indonesian military is unlikely to assuage several decades of poor military-Islamic relations. Islamic leaders in urban as well as rural areas remain highly suspicious of the military.[22] More importantly for our purposes, without a detailed study of the religious orientation of thousands of officers who have been moved through the military hierarchy during the past decade,[23] such a line of argument cannot contribute to an analysis of why the Indonesian Army has undergone accelerated waves of personnel changes during the mid-1990s.

In late 1995, a third line of analysis emerged to explain the ongoing waves of personnel promotions. Taking statements made by members of the military elite at face value, political observers and scholars alike were quick to argue that the increasingly rapid and extensive personnel reshuffles in 1995 and early 1996 were taking place in preparation for the upcoming 1997 national parliamentary elections, and that there would

---

20 The recent publication of a book written by ABRI Commander-in-Chief General Feisal Tanjung about military-Islamic relations further attests to the seriousness with which this problem is viewed. See Feisal Tanjung, *ABRI-Islam Mitra Sejati* (Jakarta: Pustaka Sinar Harapan, 1997).

21 Riza Sihbudi, "Dampak Perubahan Lingkungan Domestik Terhadap Peran Sosial Politik ABRI, " in *Peran Sospol ABRI: Masalah dan Prospeknya*, ed. Indria Samego (unpublished report, Pusat Penelitian dan Pengembangan Politik dan Kewilayahan-LIPPI, Jakarta, 1997), p. 124. This 250-page report has not been made available to the public.

22 For discussion of this, see Adam Schwarz, *A Nation in Waiting: Indonesia in the 1990s* (St. Leonards, NSW: Allen & Unwin, 1994), pp. 181, 184, 289.

23 The most extensive attempt to develop such an analysis is David Jenkins's "Islam's generals move up as the iron hoop turns green, " *Sydney Morning Herald*, January 10, 1998.

be no further changes unti_ after the election.[24] Plausible as it seemed at the time, this analysis was proven incorrect by subsequent events. Despite claims that further reassignments would not take place, the reshuffling of personnel in fact continued unabated during 1996. As we will see in chapter one, this offers telling insight into the seriousness of the structural dilemma facing the Army.

As each of these three lines of analysis reveals, observers of the Indonesian military have demonstrated a remarkable desire to interpret personnel changes in highly personalized and politicized terms. In the wake of the August 1994 wave of changes, senior military officers and civilians close to them vigorously denied that the reshuffle was "politically motivated." Retired General Rudini commented: "This isn't the first time [that there have been major personnel changes], so there's no need to relate personnel changes to political manipulations, and don't make nonsensical comments. From the time I was still Army Chief of Staff, large-scale reshuffles have happened, but journalists didn't report on them."[25]

Another contribution to our understanding of Indonesian military politics appeared in early 1997 when the LIPI held a three-day seminar titled "The Social and Political Role of ABRI." In broaching the highly sensitive issue of ABRI's role in the political process, the members of the LIPI team were quick to note that their research was initially "commissioned" by President Soeharto in 1995. On the basis of the 1995 LIPI report, and in anticipation of the 1997 general elections, Soeharto issued a Presidential decree reducing the number of seats allotted to ABRI in the People's Representative Council (DPR RI) from one hundred to seventy-five.[26] After fulfilling the President's request, the LIPI team decided to continue their research on the political role of the military, and it was the completion of their second project that provided the occasion for the highly-publicized February 1997 seminar.

LIPI research team coordinator Indria Samego explained the research

---

24 See, for example, "Soal Perubahan Pejabat Bidang Sospol: Crouch: ABRI Rapatkan Barisan, " *Merdeka*, February 24, 1996.

25 "Mutasi dalam Tubuh ABRI tak Ada Rekayasa Politik, " *Kedaulatan Rakyat*, August 15, 1994.

26 It should be noted that during the first two decades of Soeharto's rule the ABRI faction consisted of seventy-five members, the number only being raised to one hundred in 1985.

focus: "Operationally, this research will examine the development of ABRI involvement in non-military affairs and the impact that this has had."[27] It is unfortunate that the LIPI team chose to focus exclusively on the socio-political role of the military, while wholly ignoring the question of developments within the military itself. (This is perhaps understandable, however, given the difficulty of conducting such research and the obvious resistance with which any such effort would be greeted by the military elite.) In his introductory essay, Indria Samego simply notes that ABRI's social-political role has a direct impact on its internal dynamics.

> The negative impact of ABRI's [socio-political] role on its own internal workings is reflected in a number of tendencies: the repressive attitude of the military, the weakness of military professionalism, declining discipline, deterioration in ABRI's ability to face foreign military threats, the misuse of power, neglecting to develop the military, and siding with particular social groups so as to benefit the military.[28]

This theme is reiterated throughout the report, with repeated suggestions that the military's socio-political role has had an adverse effect on military professionalism.[29] The resulting policy recommendations made by the LIPI team were, in their own words, a call "for ABRI to reduce its involvement in practical political activity and to respond more positively to [societal] demands for democracy."[30]

Each of the above approaches to the study of the Indonesian military offers its own insights and illuminates aspects of the ongoing negotiations between the military and political elites. But as this brief discussion suggests, we believe that existing analyses of the Indonesian military and its role in national politics cannot fully explain the increasing frequency of large-scale personnel reshuffles. By focusing on personalities, personal connections, and cliques in the military elite, each of these

---

27 Indria Samego, "Demokratisasi Peran Sosial Politik ABRI: Catatan Pendahuluan, " in *Peran Sospol ABRI*, p. 24. This 250-page report has not been made available to the public.

28 Ibid., p. 27.

29 Ibid., pp. 192, 201, 221.

30 See "ABRI: Redefinisi, Bukan ke Tangsi, " *Tiras*, March 13, 1997, p. 85; and the interview with LIPI team leader Indria Samego, " Negara Ini Tidak Ada Kelas, " *Sinar*, March 8, 1997, p. 17.

approaches over-politicizes the internal dynamics of the military while underestimating the significance of structural forces operating within the Army itself. To be satisfactory, an analysis of the internal dynamics of the Indonesian military during the 1990s must be able to answer two basic questions. First, why have personnel changes in the Army accelerated during the 1990s? Second, how are decisions made regarding personnel in the Indonesian military? This study was originally designed to provide an answer to these two questions. The dramatic events leading up to Soeharto's resignation on May 21, 1998 raises additional puzzles about military politics. If Soeharto relied on the appointment of relatives and officers known to be loyal to him, why then didn't the military elite defend the embattled dictator? If, as many observers have argued, the Army is deeply divided, then why has it remained united in the face of Soeharto's fall? The long-term worth of this study will also be measured by the extent to which it can provide a framework within which to answer these more recent questions.

STUDYING MILITARY POLITICS IN NEW ORDER INDONESIA

The study of military politics is difficult under most circumstances. As one author has commented, "almost all scholars who write on the military preface their work by noting the limitations in material and data."[31] Militaries have good reason to safeguard information about both their inner workings and their activities in the domestic and international spheres. There is little to be gained from openness, and often a great deal to lose. And the catch-all issue of "national security" provides most militaries with a ready-made justification for secrecy.

It is, in large part, the limited nature of available data about militaries that has led scholars to focus on questions of ideology. The central tenet of Indonesian military ideology is the concept of *dwifungsi*, or dual function, according to which the functions of the military involve both national defense and involvement in sociopolitical affairs. While there have been extended debates about the original intent and scope of this

---

31 Mary Patricia Callahan, "The Origins of Military Rule in Burma" (PhD dissertation, Cornell University, 1996).

concept, one recent work concluded with the penetrating observation that "ABRI's *dwi fungsi* [sic] is in reality only one function —the maintenance of national stability..."[32] We believe that it is essential to move beyond questions about the military's formal ideology and to address changing dynamics within the military as an institution and the shifting nature of civil-military relations in Indonesia.

Despite claims about the scarcity of data, there is more information readily available about ABRI than is commonly assumed. The Indonesian military has published officially commissioned histories of the revolution and the military, policy manuals and institutional handbooks, commemorative albums and yearbooks, and histories of commands and campaigns against regional rebellions. Individual officers have written additional (and at times alternative) histories, biographies, and memoirs. The Armed Forces also publish and own a number of daily and monthly newspapers. The most important of these include the national *Harian Umum Angkatan Bersenjata* (Armed Forces Daily) and a monthly paper, *Sapta Marga*, devoted to internal military news.

The daily and monthly reports in these and other newspapers provide a wealth of data on individual Army officers. Large-scale waves of senior personnel changes are covered in great depth, with detailed information about the officers and posts involved. News magazines frequently print biographical sketches of prominent or rising officers along with lengthy interviews. It is common for newspapers to carry articles about the transfer and appointment of officers. Information culled from newspapers and magazines provides the basis for this monograph. These data cover an estimated 25 percent of all officers who graduated from the National Military Academy over two and a half decades, as well as both non-academy graduates and non-commissioned officers. We have ABRI to thank for making this wealth of information available to the public.

In analyzing these data, we have employed a number of simple statistical methods. These are used to explore such phenomena as changing command tenure at various levels, succession patterns, variations in officers' tours of duty over time, career paths, age trends, and the relative

---

32 MacFarling, *The Dual Function of the Indonesian Armed Forces*, Preface (no page number).

success of cohorts from the military academy. Several of the methods are new not only to the study of the Indonesian military,[33] but to the field of military politics in general. Because of its psychological importance in military culture, several authors have examined the length of time that it takes officers to "make" (or be promoted in) rank.[34] But while promotions in rank may only occur at five, six, or even seven year intervals, officers commonly serve in more than one post at a given rank. In an effort to move beyond the limitations imposed by rank-based analysis, we have focused on the length of tenure of officers at different positions within the Army. This allows us to be more sensitive to short-term change within the officer corps than is possible with a purely rank-based approach. In the course of this study, we wish to see if and how the use of statistical methods brings new light to bear on both the internal dynamics of the Army and civil-military relations in Indonesia.

OVERVIEW

This is a study of the internal dynamics of the Indonesian Army in the decade and a half leading up to the fall of Soeharto. While the empirical analysis is limited to the Army, the findings have implications for the military as a whole. Throughout the work, we use the word Army when referring to the single service branch, and the terms "ABRI," "Armed Forces," and "military" interchangeably to refer to the four service branches together.

Chapter one examines change in the Army officer corps during the 1980s and 1990s. In contrast to the existing literature, it argues that the increasing frequency of large scale reshuffles of military personnel was primarily neither a response to particular political developments nor the product of individual personalities and cliques. We argue instead that this was a reflection of changes in the size of the officer corps. Tracing these changes to the National Military Academy in Magelang, Central Java, we

---

33 The only known attempt to apply statistical methods to the study of the Indonesian military is MacFarling's recent book. This, however, is based on a curiously skewed database of "771 TNI-AD (Army) officers of brigadier rank and above, some of whom had served from World War Two onwards." Ibid., p. 9.

34 The best of these is Robin Luckham's *The Nigerian Military: A Sociological Analysis of Authority and Revolt, 1960-1967* (Cambridge: Cambridge University Press, 1971).

demonstrate that many of the current changes taking place in the Army are a result of internal structural features of the Army.

Chapter two explores the career patterns of Army officers during the 1990s. Through a detailed analysis of succession patterns and the examination of class cohorts from the National Military Academy, this chapter further refines the basic model presented in chapter one. This analysis highlights several forms of institutional rationalization within the Army during the late Soeharto era.

Drawing on the macro-level analysis of the Army officer corps in the preceding chapters, chapter three discusses the political implications of these structural changes for military rule in Indonesia. While the changing size of the officer corps has presented the Army with certain new opportunities, it has also raised new conflicts and tensions. Primary among these are questions of changing career prospects, alterations in the nature of the military and its ability to continue its direct role in socio-political affairs, and emerging divisions between active and retired officers.

CHAPTER ONE
OUT OF MAGELANG

Professional militaries are premised on adherence to fixed policies and known bureaucratic norms. Particularly important are the rules governing the assignment, rotation, and promotion of officers. During three decades of Soeharto's rule, the Indonesian military traditionally announced major waves of personnel changes among commissioned Army officers around the time of the August 17 Independence Day celebration and the October 5 Armed Forces Day ceremony. The regularity of these announcements contributed to stable expectations among the officer corps about the process of assignments and the chain of command within the Army.

During the 1990s, however, the frequency and scope of major personnel reshuffles within the Indonesian Army increased markedly. In early 1992, in the wake of the Santa Cruz massacre in Dili, East Timor, the sacking of several prominent generals stimulated a first wave of personnel changes. This was followed in mid-1992 by the replacement of all top Army leaders, the largest single overhaul of the officer corps since the mid-1980s. Only just completed, these changes were followed in April and August 1993 by further waves of personnel changes under the direction of the short-tenured Commander-in-Chief General Edi Sudradjat. The following year, 1994, saw two more major waves of personnel changes, one in January at Armed Forces headquarters and the other in August within the Army high command. The most sweeping set of transfers to date came in early 1995, involving wholesale personnel changes at the Armed Forces headquarters and the Army central and regional commands. In short, between 1992 and 1994, major personnel changes among the military elite took place twice a year. Over the next two years this frequency increased sharply. In 1995, there were five major personnel transfers. And in 1996, there were another four large-scale reshuffles of Army officers.

Observers of the Indonesian military were quick to note this increase in the number of annual personnel rotations. They also speculated about the possible causes of this increase. Among the explanations commonly cited are tensions between the Presidential Palace and the Army elite,[1] concern about the military's relations with Islamic leaders,[2] and preparations for the 1997-98 legislative and presidential elections.[3] Despite the focus on the increasing frequency of personnel rotations, little attention has been paid either to internal military norms or the political consequences of these personnel changes. And yet, the increase in transfers holds significant implications for the tenure of staff and command officers in the Indonesian Army and for Indonesian politics in general.

The issue of command tenure is an old problem for the Indonesian military. During the transformation from a guerrilla to a standing military during the late 1950s, the military elite was faced with the problem of regularizing promotions and standardizing the length of assignments. One of the more important measures taken at the time was to institute and secure acceptance among the officer corps of a standard two-year tour of duty for Army officers.[4] Curiously, during the New Order there has been little if any discussion about a standard tour of duty.[5] One of the few, oblique official statements about this came at the time of the 1985 Army reorganization. In response to questions about Army officers being seconded to serve in civilian posts, Army Chief of Staff General Rudini explained that if an active-duty officer were to serve for two consecutive five-year terms, he would miss three opportunities "to be promoted" (*naik jabatan*).[6] Taken at face value, this implies an expectation that Army

---

1   The Editors, "Current Data on the Indonesian Military Elite: September 1, 1993 - August 31, 1994, " *Indonesia* 58 (October 1994): 84.

2   See, for example, "Dua Jenderal Santri Di Pucuk Piramida ABRI" and "Abri dan Islam, " *Tiras*, February 23, 1995, pp. 55-59.

3   "Soal Perubahan Pejabat Bidang Sospol: Crouch: ABRI Rapatkan Barisan, " *Merdeka*, February 24, 1996; and "Pergantian Pimpinan ABRI mengantisipasi Pemilu 1997, " *Kompas*, March 11, 1996.

4   Ruth McVey, "The Post-Revolutionary Transformation of the Indonesian Army, " Part II, *Indonesia* 13 (April 1972): 150.

5   Lowry notes that during the New Order "the officer promotion and posting cycle has been institutionalized and regularised, " but does not provide details. Robert Lowry, *The Armed Forces of Indonesia* (St. Leonards, NSW: Allen & Unwin, 1996), p. 124.

6   "Dwifungsi setelah Reorganisasi, " *Tempo*, May 11, 1995, p. 13. In the same interview, Rudini

officers should serve a three-year tour of duty in any given post. During a 1997 seminar on the military in Yogyakarta, now-retired General Rudini offered the most explicit statement to date: "…in the military the minimum tour of duty in one position should be three years, the maximum four years. But if there is a vacuum because of mistakes in development or the management of personnel, it is possible for jumps to take place."[7]

Despite the silence of the military elite regarding the tour of duty for officers, the Indonesian press frequently comments on the length of tenure of officers at the time of rotations and new appointments, voicing surprise or raising eyebrows when officers are replaced after a conspicuously short tour of duty, and noting stability when an officer serves for a particularly long time. It is not uncommon, however, for territorial commanders themselves to comment that it is time they be replaced. These remarks appear not as requests for reassignment or promotion, but as acknowledgment of military norms and rationality.[8]

In this chapter, we provide a statistical analysis of changing command tenure for key command positions in the Indonesian Army. First, we find a significant decline in the length of tenure of commanding Army officers at all territorial and combat levels. Second, we argue that the decline in tenure of Army officers is the result of an increase in the size of the officer corps graduating from the National Military Academy (Akademi Militer Nasional; AMN) in the late 1960s and from its successor, Akabri, in the early 1970s. Finally, in light of these findings we reevaluate the personnel changes leading up to the 1997 legislative election and 1998 session of the MPR.

CHANGING COMMAND TENURE IN THE ARMY OFFICER CORPS

On the basis of data collected from the Indonesian press over a ten-year period, it is possible to calculate mean tenure of staff and command officers in the Indonesian Army.[9] For the sake of simplicity, the following analysis

---

mentioned there being a "minimum" and "maximum" tour of duty for each position, but did not specify their lengths.

7 We are grateful to Made Tony Supriatma for providing the transcript from the seminar.

8 See, for example, the comments by Kodam V Brawijaya (East Java) commander Major General Imam Oetomo in "Pangdam: Sudah waktunya saya diganti, " *Surya*, June 12, 1997.

9 The primary source of information on active officers, rotations, and new appointments has been

will be limited to tenure for territorial and battalion commanders.[10] Nevertheless, we expect that similar patterns will be found among staff officers as well. The mean tenure for command positions in any month was computed as the average tenure of all officers serving in that position for at least one day during that month.[11] As will be noted, there is considerable variation in the sample size for different commands: the most representative sample is for posts held by high ranking officers, and the least representative sample for Military District (Kodim) and battalion commanders. This reflects both the relative political importance of these positions and the availability of data.

Kodam Commanders

The largest territorial unit of the Indonesian Army is the Regional Military Command (Komando Daerah Militer; Kodam), the commander of which (*Panglima Kodam*; Pangdam) is a two-star general. Though far less powerful than they were in the 1950s, these commanders are among the most politically important officers in the Indonesian military. In 1985, then Commander-in-Chief L. B. (Benny) Moerdani, reconfigured the existing sixteen Kodam into ten larger units (see Map 1.1). At the time, Moerdani noted that this reorganization was necessary because there were not a sufficient number of qualified officers to serve as Kodam commanders: "The public may not be aware that it is difficult to find sixteen Kodam commanders every three or four years. If you look only at the list [of officers], it might seem easy."[12] Explicit in this statement is Moerdani's conception of the appropriate tenure for Kodam commanders —three or four years.

But have tenure trends for commanding officers in fact corresponded

---

the military newspaper *Angkatan Bersenjata*. This has been supplemented with news from a host of national as well as regional newspapers and magazines.

10 We have omitted the brigades and divisions under Kostrad because the extremely small numbers of commanding officers make statistical analysis of questionable use.

11 These calculations are based on only those officers for whom the date of both appointment to and transfer from a given command position are known. In cases where the month of appointment or transfer is known but not the day, we have used the first day of the month as the basis of calculation.

12 Interview with Benny Moerdani, "ABRI Tahun 2000 Seperti Apa?" *Tempo*, May 4, 1995, pp. 16-17.

to Moerdani's conception and intentions? As illustrated in Figure 1.1, the tenure of Kodam commanders has passed through three distinct periods.[13] In the immediate aftermath of the 1985 reorganization of the military, the mean tenure for the ten Kodam commanders was slightly over two years, significantly lower than Moerdani's stated model. Beginning in mid-1988, the length of tenure for Kodam commanders increased sharply, peaking at three years in 1990. In early 1991, however, tenure began a steep decline, leveling off in 1993 at a mere one and a half years per commander.[14] Finally, in mid-1997 the tenure for Kodam commanders again drops sharply, falling to a mere 350 days per officer.[15] Although this sudden decrease began under Feisal Tanjung's term, its explanation lies not with Feisal but rather with the fall of Soeharto and the housecleaning and consolidation of power carried out by ABRI Commander-in-Chief General Wiranto.[16] The extraordinarily low command tenure of the late-1997 and early-1998 period is institutionally untenable for ABRI over a long period, and we fully expect the current command line-up to serve significantly longer tours of duty and for tenure to increase over the next several years.

---

13 Because of their political importance and the small number of positions involved, the installation of new Kodam commanders is almost always reported in the press. The data in Table 1.1 are based on identification of tenure for all officers who served as a Kodam commander from 1985 until the present (excluding current office-holders). Unfortunately, it has not been possible to extend the analysis back prior to 1985. A preliminary (but statistically inferior) version of this analysis appeared in The Editors, "The Indonesian Military in the Mid-1990s: Political Maneuvering or Structural Change?" *Indonesia* 63 (April 1997): 91-106.

14 The relationship between the tenure of Kodam commanders and ABRI leadership is discussed in Appendix 1.1.

15 The 1998 trend was calculated based on the those officers (nine individuals) who had each completed his tour of duty as Kodam commander as of June 1998; one Kodam commander, who was appointed in August 1997 and who continued to serve at the time of writing, has been excluded from these calculations.

16 This was compounded by the death of Major General Yudomo SHD in a helicopter crash in Baucau, East Timor, a mere nine days after his appointment as commander of Kodam IX Udayana.

Map 1.1

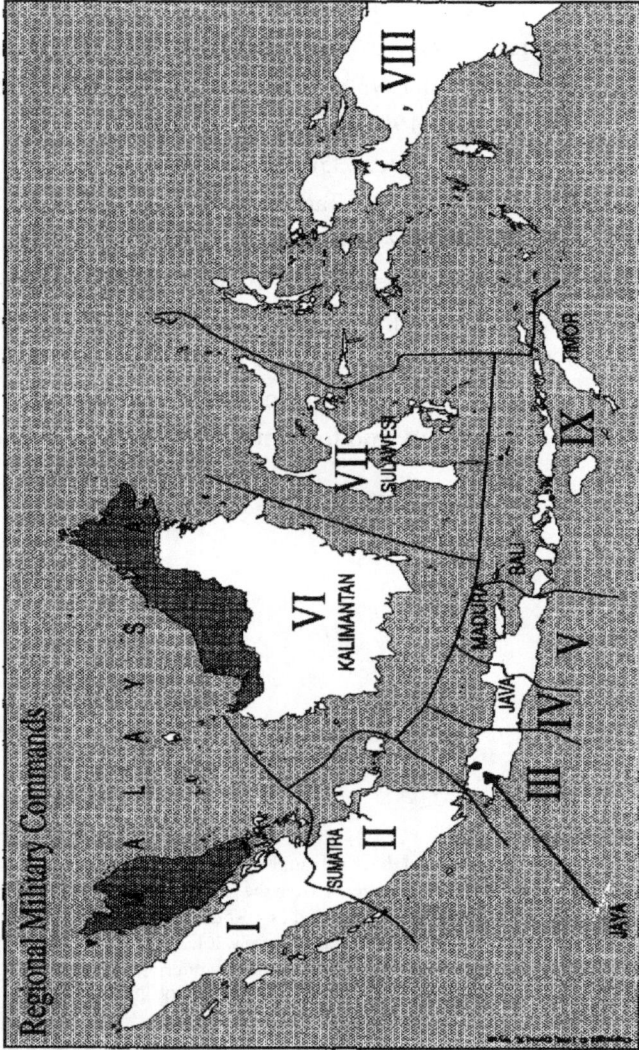

Regional Military Commands

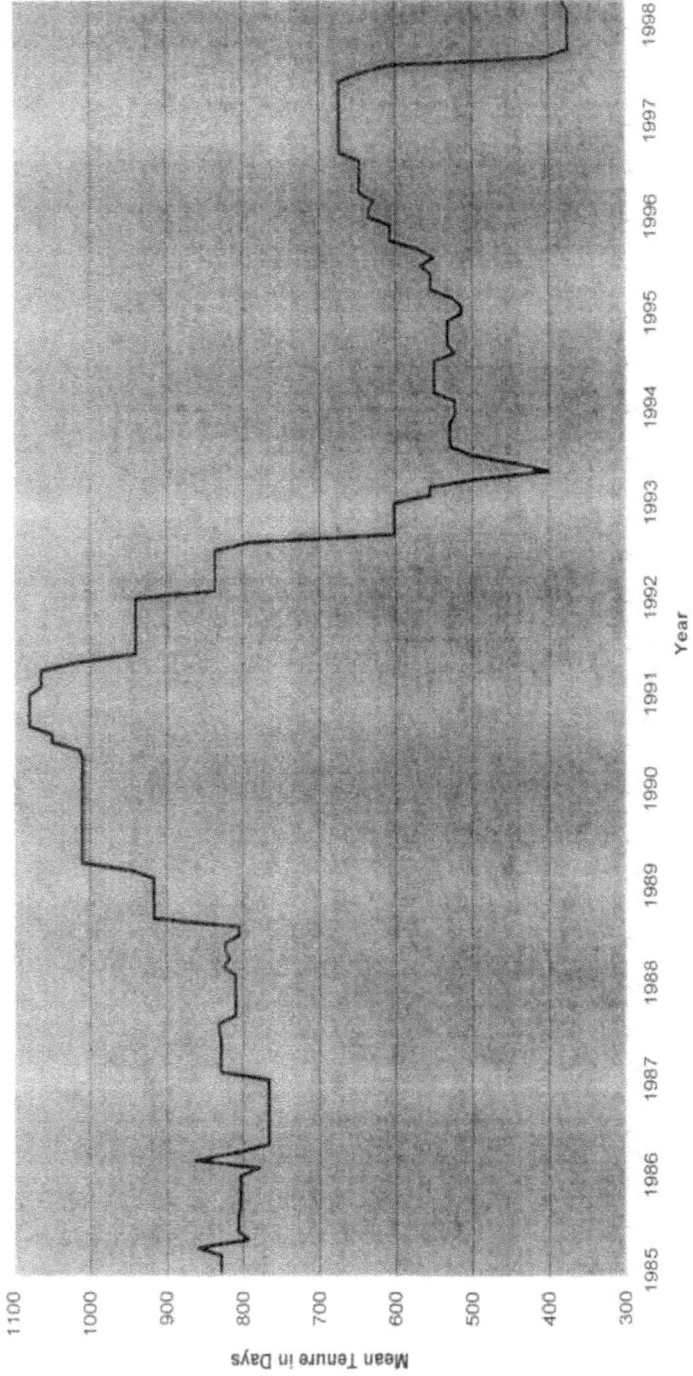

Figure 1.1: Mean Tenure for Kodam Commanders (1985-1998)

Korem Commanders

Each Kodam consists of four to six Sub-Regional Military Commands (Komando Resort Militer; Korem), headed by an officer with the rank of colonel. In all, there are thirty-nine Korem,[17] those on Java corresponding roughly to the old colonial residencies, most of those outside of Java corresponding to provinces.[18] Each Korem oversees territorial security and is responsible for the activities of lower-ranking District Military Commands (Kodim) and one or more territorial combat battalions.

The Korem were central to General Moerdani's plan for the new-look Army. At the time of the 1985 Army reorganization, Moerdani noted that the newly reconstituted Korem would serve as the "meritocratic breeding-ground of future military leaders of the nation."[19] This being the case, one would assume there to be a degree of regularity in the staffing and tenure of these posts. Unfortunately the military elite has not offered any comments about the targeted tour of duty for Korem commanders, and we therefore lack a baseline against which to compare the tenure trends over the past decade.

The mean tenure of Korem commanders from 1985 until the present is plotted in Figure 1.2.[20] Once again, we find that the tenure of Korem commanders is marked by distinct episodes. Unlike the tenure for Kodam commanders, however, these periods do not correspond neatly to the command of different Pangabs. Immediately following Moerdani's reorganization, tenure for Korem commanders averaged roughly

---

17 During the 1990s, there has been scattered talk about increasing the number of Korem. See, for example, "Kodam IV/Diponegoro segera membentuk Korem Baru, " *Angkatan Bersenjata*, July 7, 1995. After much discussion, in 1998 two new Korem were created within Kodam Jaya (Jakarta), bringing the total number of Korem to forty-one. See "Aneka Berita, " *Suara Pembaruan*, October 29, 1998.

18 On the relationship between the Army's territorial commands and the civil administration, see Benedict Anderson, "Current Data on the Indonesian Military Elite, " *Indonesia* 40 (October 1985): 134-135.

19 Quoted in Benedict Anderson, "Current Data on the Indonesian Military Elite, " *Indonesia* 48 (October 1989): 67-68. Full analysis of the importance of Korem command in determining future military leadership would require evaluating the career trajectories of the more than three-hundred officers who have served as Korem commanders since the 1985 reforms, a task that exceeds data constraints. For a preliminary discussion, see chapter two.

20 This graph is based on identification of tenure for 275 of the 340 officers (80 percent) known to have served as Korem commanders between 1985 and the present (excluding current office holders).

nine hundred days per officer. During 1987, mean command tenure plummeted 30 percent from over one thousand days to around seven hundred days per officer.[21] Over the following four years tenure rose marginally, peaking at an average of eight hundred days in January 1991. In 1992, Korem command tenure began a second prolonged decline, falling to a mere five hundred days per commander by early 1995. All told, during the decade 1985-1995, Korem command tenure declined by about 45 percent. Since 1995, tenure has risen from five hundred days to over 650 days, an increase of approximately 30 percent.[22]

This evidence of reduced tenure for Korem commanders over the past several years strongly suggests that the strictly "meritocratic", promotional policy introduced by General Moerdani has not in fact been implemented. Rather, a case can be made that the shortened length of tenure means that Korem commanders are being given less time in which to master fully the particular responsibilities and challenges of their positions and, consequently, that the Army elite has even less basis on which to evaluate meritocratically these officers' performances.

Finally, it is essential to note that there is a clear relationship between the changing tenure of Kodam and Korem commanders. For example, we can identify officers who served as Korem commanders during the 1985-87 period, at which time average tenure was between nine hundred and one thousand days per officer. Some of these same officers were appointed as Kodam commanders three to four years later, again serving nine hundred to one thousand days on average. Similarly, theofficers who served as Korem commanders during the 1988-91 period had significantly shorter terms than their predecessors. When members of this cohort were appointed as Kodam commanders beginning in 1992, they served correspondingly reduced terms once again.[23]

---

21 Although tenure for Java-based Korem commanders dropped earlier and to a lower level than for Korem commanders in the outer islands, by 1989 the two converged and have remained virtually identical throughout the 1990s. For this and a comparison of trouble/operations and non-operations areas, see Appendices 1.2 and 1.3.

22 This recent increase is likely to be understated because the sample does not include long-serving officers who have not yet completed their current tours of duty as Korem commanders. This also applies to the figures for other command positions.

23 This correspondence between Korem and Kodam command tenure is illustrated graphically in Appendices 1.4 and 1.5.

Figure 1.2: Mean Tenure for Korem Commanders
(1985-1997)

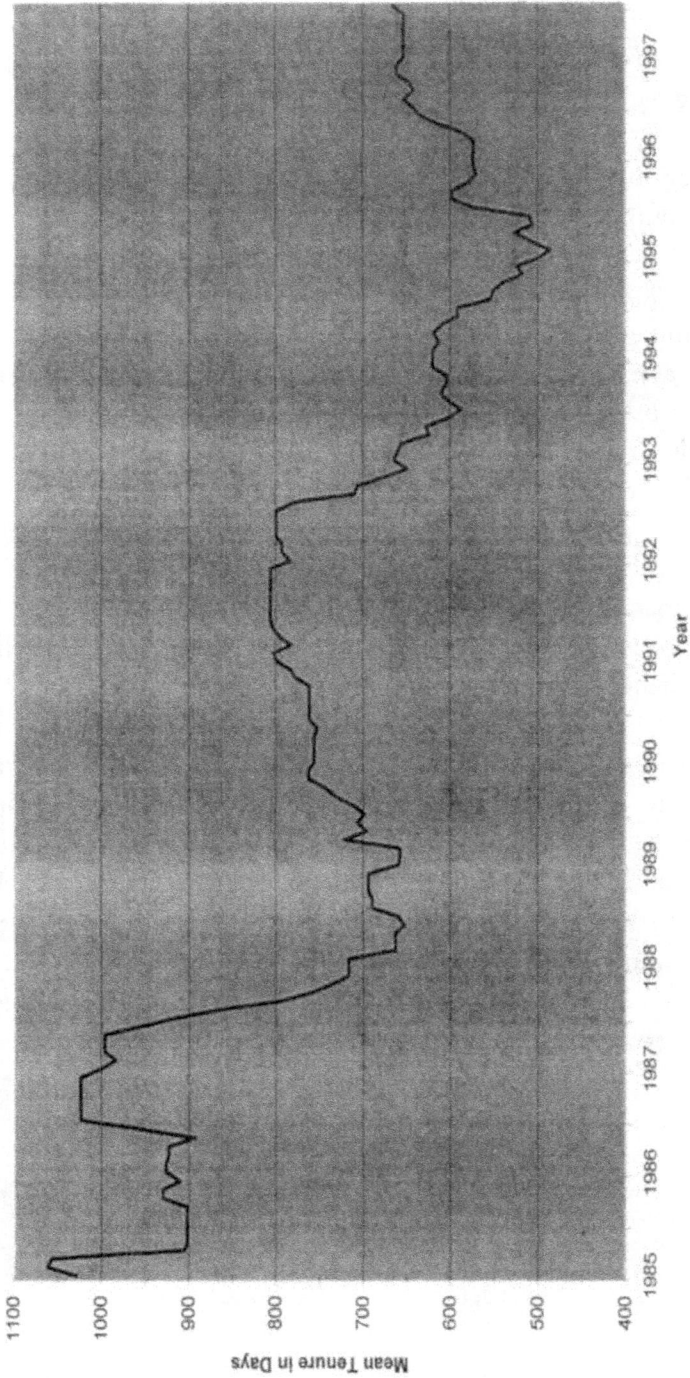

Kodim Commanders

Below the Korem, there are approximately 280 District Military Commands (*Komando Distrik Militer; Kodim*) in Indonesia,[24] each commanded by an officer with the rank of lieutenant colonel. Corresponding to the civilian administrative district (*kabupaten*), Kodim have a relatively limited staff and do not oversee combat troops.[25] Although the large number of Kodim makes statistical analysis of tenure trends more difficult than for Kodam or Korem commanders, such analysis is perhaps most important at this level. In part this is because the Kodim constitute the first rung in the extensive apparatus responsible for overseeing security and preventing civil disturbances. More importantly, the Kodim are the lowest level territorial unit normally commanded by commissioned officers who have graduated from the military academy, and tenure trends at this level thus provide telltale signs of changing career prospects.[26]

The data in Figure 1.3 show that tenure for Kodim commanders has decreased steadily during the 1990s.[27] While mean tenure rose marginally between 1989 and late 1990, peaking at a high of nine hundred days per commander, it has plummeted since, falling to under six hundred days

---

24 In 1992 there were 279 Kodim. See "Predikat terbaik untuk sebuah kepedulian, " *Angkatan Bersenjata*, January 9, 1992. The number has increased marginally over the past five years with the formation of several new Kodim (in Bengkulu, Bitung, and Timika, for example).

25 Kodim are reported to have about fifty personnel; they supervise Sub-District Military Commands (Komando Rayon Militer; Koramil), commanded by junior officers or senior non-commissioned officers. Lowry, *The Armed Forces of Indonesia*, pp. 229-230. During the early 1980s ABRI is reported to have discussed allowing Akabri (Akademi Angkatan Bersenjata Republik Indonesia; Armed Forces Academy of the Republic of Indonesia) graduates to serve as Koramil commanders, though we have not been able to document such a case. See David Jenkins, *Suharto and His Generals: Indonesian Military Politics 1975-1983* (Ithaca, NY: Cornell Modern Indonesia Project, 1984), p. 46.

26 It is important to note, however, that the position of Kodim commander is not restricted to military academy graduates. Non-academy graduates who attend Officer Cadet School (Sekolah Calon Perwira; Secapa) in Bandung and reach the rank of lieutenant colonel may also compete for these positions. The officer corps is also supplemented by the recruitment of tertiary graduates who, according to Lowry, "can compete with Akabri graduates for unit command and promotion to the highest ranks." Lowry, *The Armed Forces of Indonesia*, p. 118; and "Alumni Secapa punya kesempatan bersaing dan prospektif, " *Angkatan Bersenjata*, July 1, 1997. These policies have important implications, to which we will return later.

27 Due to data limitations, this analysis must be limited to the 1989-1997 period. Figure 1.3 is based on data covering the tenure of 151 Kodim commanders who served between 1989 and the present. Assuming a two-year tour of duty as the army norm, this sample represents approximately 12 percent of the total number of Kodim commanders during the period in question. The analysis of changing tenure must be viewed in light of the limited nature of this sample.

in early 1996. Since then, command tenure has stabilized at six hundred days.[28] As this report from a newspaper in Central Java indicates, some local commanders had set even lower limits on command tenure:

> When contacted by *Bernas* on Saturday, Brigadier General Soemarsono said that in August all Kodim commanders in the Surakarta region who have served for more than one year will be replaced. This is part of the process of regeneration [*regenerasi*] that has been taking place naturally [*alamiah*].[29]

Although it would be difficult to test using available statistical data, there appears to be a general trend for command tenure to be shortest in the largest urban centers (one to two years) and longest in rural areas (two to four years). Assignment as Kodim commander in the urban centers of Jakarta, Semarang, Surabaya, and Medan is generally a sign of a rising career. After one and a half to two years of service, such an officer can expect to be promoted to serve as a deputy assistant to the chief of staff of a Kodam or as chief of staff to a Korem commander in the same region. By contrast, assignment as Kodim commander in a rural area is as likely as not to last for two to four years and signal career stagnation. Following such a long posting in a rural backwater, the best that a Kodim commander can hope for would be a civilian posting as *Bupati* (Regent) or *Walikota* (Mayor), though it is more common for such officers to be appointed to the local legislature (DPRD).[30]

---

28 As is the case for Korem commanders, the calculations for 1996-1997 are probably lower than the actual mean.

29 "Kol Inf. Sriyanto Danrem 074/Warastratama, " *Bernas*, September 2, 1997.

30 These patterns are more fully discussed in chapter two.

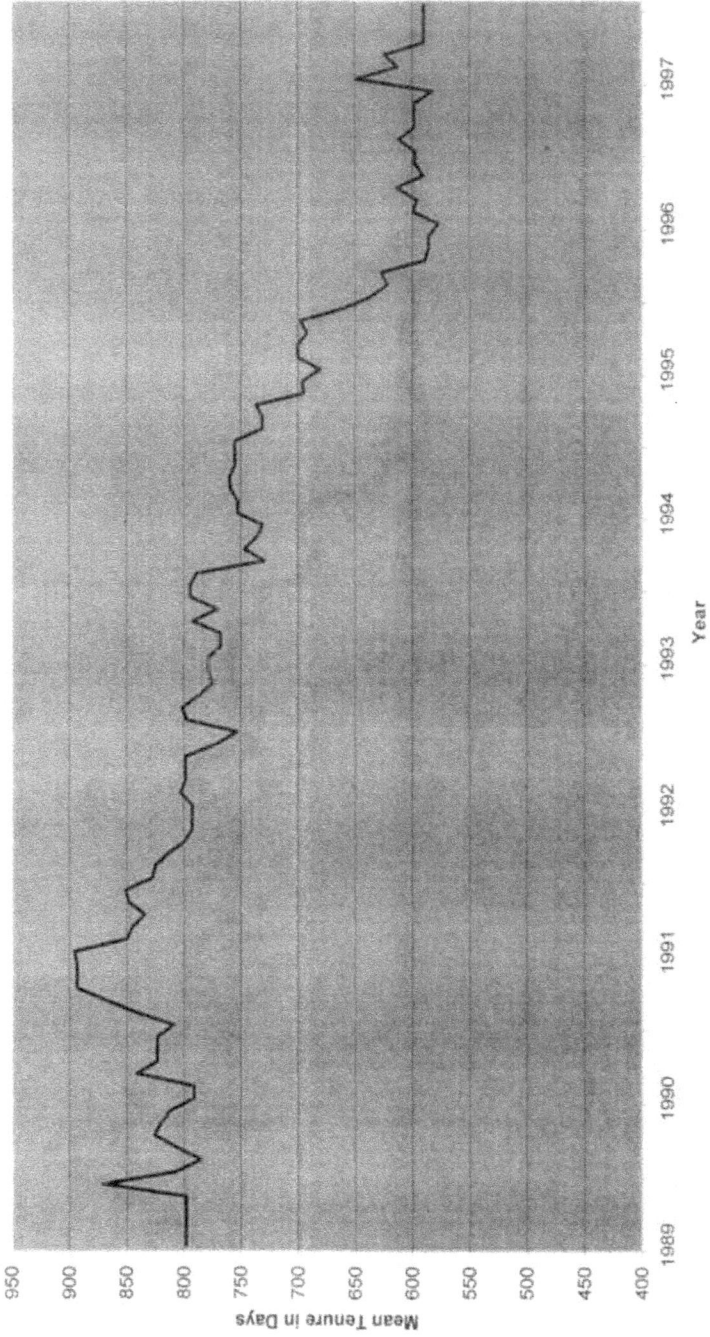

Figure 1.3: Mean Tenure for Kodim Commanders (1989-1997)

Battalion Commanders

There are two kinds of battalions in the Indonesian Army. First, each Kodam has a number of associated battalions representing the different service specializations within the Army (e.g. infantry, cavalry, anti-aircraft, etc.). Commanded by a major or lieutenant colonel, these are the real troops behind the Army's territorial structure. In addition to these territorially based units, there are also battalions under the Special Forces Command (Komando Pasukan Khusus; Kopassus) and Army Strategic Command (Komando Strategis Angkatan Darat; Kostrad).[31] In all, there are reported to be 128 battalions in Indonesia.[32]

As was the case with Kodim commanders, it is relatively uncommon for newspapers to report on the change of battalion commanders, and the available sample from which to calculate command tenure is limited.[33] Figure 1.4 shows that the tenure of battalion commanders has undergone a steady decline over the last eight years: from a high of about 850 days during 1990-91, average tenure fell to a mere five hundred days per commander in 1996.[34] Remarkably, despite the limited sample size, the tenure trend for battalion commanders is virtually identical to that for Kodim commanders. The only difference between the two is that while tenure for Kodim commanders began to increase in early 1996, that for battalion commanders has continued to drop. It remains to be seen whether, in the near future, the tenure trend for battalion commanders will continue to fall or, more likely, resemble that for Kodim commanders and increase in duration.

---

31 Kopassus is divided into five administrative groups (two based in Jakarta, one each in Serang, Batujajar, and Surakarta) and, according to the latest reports, four specialized battalions. Kostrad is divided into two infantry divisions (one based in Jakarta and one in Malang), with battalions stationed in second-tier cities throughout Java. No information is available on tenure of Kopassus battalion commanders, though data for Kostrad battalion commanders is quite good.

32 "Jajaran ABRI agar tingkatkan kepedulian sosial, " *Angkatan Bersenjata*, July 6, 1992. The figures provided by Lowry differ: he counts ninety-five territorial battalions, forty Kostrad battalions, and four Kopassus covert warfare battalions. See Lowry, *The Armed Forces of Indonesia*, pp. 230-232.

33 For the 1990-1997 period, exact tenure data are available for fifty-seven battalion commanders; these represent an estimated 10 percent of the total number of officers who served as battalion commanders during this period. Due to data limitations, this analysis cannot be extended before 1990.

34 Again, the calculations for 1996-1997 are likely somewhat understated. Note that the drop in tenure between 1990 and 1995, for which the data are more robust, is significant in and of itself.

Figure 1.4: Mean Tenure for Battalion Commanders
(1989-1997)

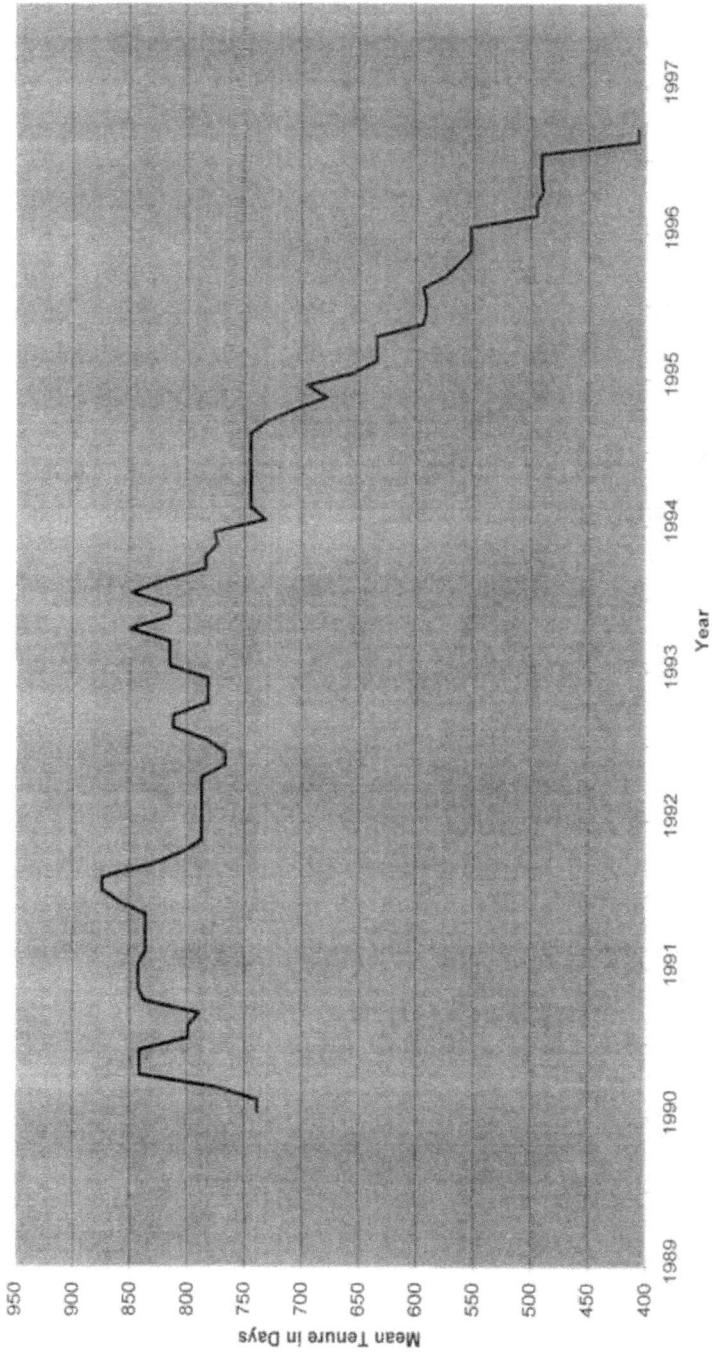

A STRUCTURAL EXPLANATION

How, then, are we to explain the increasingly frequent transfer of senior as well as middle-ranking military officers during the 1990s? What explains the correspondingly dramatic drop in command tenure at all levels within the Indonesian Army over the past decade? As previously discussed, most observers have interpreted the acceleration of large-scale personnel rotations in terms of current political concerns. Conflicts among senior officers and the President, issues of security surrounding the 1997-98 elections, and post-succession political posturing in Jakarta were all clearly important developments. But none of these lines of approach satisfactorily addresses the structural changes that took place within the Army officer corps. We believe that the answer to this puzzle does not lie primarily in Jakarta in the mid-1990s, but rather in Magelang, Central Java, home of the National Military Academy, some three decades ago.

The National Military Academy (AMN)[35] was established in 1957 as part of then-Army Chief of Staff General Nasution's ongoing effort to turn a regionally based guerrilla Army into a professional as well as national military.[36] Inducted in 1957, the first AMN class totaling fifty-nine officers graduated three years later in 1960. The following three AMN classes (1961-1963) averaged 125 graduates each. During the next several years both the intake of cadets and the size of graduating AMN classes varied widely. In 1964, Class 5 totaled 280 officers. In 1965 there was another sharp rise, with Class 6 graduating 433 officers. Curiously, the number of graduates then fell to an average of 220 officers in 1966 and 1967. In 1968 class size again peaked with Class 9 graduating 465 officers. Because of the institutional shift introduced in 1965 from a three to a four-year educational program, no class graduated in 1969.[37] Although class size

---

35 The AMN in Magelang has gone through several incarnations. In December 1965 it was renamed Akademi Angkatan Bersenjata Republik Indonesia (Akabri) and made responsible for the education of all four service branches. In 1972 separate service academies were re-established, with that for the Army renamed Akademi Militer. We will use the specific name when referring to a particular period, but will use the gloss "military academy" when referring to the academy over time.

36 McVey, "The Post-Revolutionary Transformation of the Indonesian Army, " Part I, *Indonesia* 11 (April 1971): 131-176, and Part II, *Indonesia* 13 (April 1972): 147-182.

37 This was accompanied by a change of name from Akademi Militer Nasional to Akademi Militer ABRI (Armed Forces Academy of the Republic of Indonesia; Akabri).

continued to fluctuate, between 1970 and 1975 Akabri graduated an average of nearly four hundred officers per year (see Table 1.1).

Table 1.1:

Army Cadets Graduated from the National Military Academy, 1960-1991

Class Number	Year of Graduation	Military Academy Graduates	Class Number	Year of Graduation	Military Academy Graduates
1	1960	59	16	1976	85
2	1961	151	17	1977	79
3	1962	112	18	1978	93
4	1963	113	19	1979	no class
5	1964	280	20	1980	102
6	1965	433	21	1981	146
7	1966	243	22	1982	85
8	1967	203	23	1983	184
9	1968	465	24	1984	244
	1969	no class	25	1985	254
10	1970	437	26	1986	227
11	1971	329	27	1987	278
12	1972	389	28	1988	276[a]
13	1973	436	29	1989	247
14	1974	434	30	1990	267
15	1975	304	31	1991	281

[a] Two classes are listed for this year, one with 276 graduates, the second with 264 graduates. We have been unable to verify the correct total.
Source: *Daftar Alumni Akademi Militer 1948-1996.*

There is no official explanation for the sharp increase in the size of AMN classes during the 1960s. Publications on the AMN (by the military as well as by scholars) cover the founding of the academy, requirements for admission, educational principles, and the curriculum, but wholly neglect issues of class size and the equally important issue of the social background of cadets admitted.[38] The silence of the Army and military elite on questions of class size at the military academy and the total size of the commissioned officer corps is puzzling, to say the least.[39] In an early version of this work, it was suggested that the increase in AMN class size might have been a response to the challenges posed by Sukarno's Confrontation (*Konfrontasi*) with Malaysia and the perceived need for a greater number of combat officers; we now think that this was mistaken.[40]

An alternative, if partial, explanation for this sharp increase in academy intake is suggested by Ian MacFarling in his recent book. MacFarling writes: "In the past the Army has specifically recruited cadets into the Military Academy for the *karyawan* [seconded to civil service] role. The TNI-AD [Army] class of 1973 was 400 strong and when questioned why it was so large a member of the graduating class remarked that the aim was that many of the graduates would fill karyawan posts."[41] Intriguing as this explanation is, we find it unlikely that the Army would admit many more cadets than it needs for active service, and thus risk upsetting the balance within the officer corps, simply in order to have more officers available to be seconded to civilian posts.

---

38 See Mako Akabri, *Sejarah Akademi Angkatan Bersenjata RI (1945-1971)*, two volumes (1993); Peter Britton, "Military Professionalism in Indonesia: Javanese and Western Military Traditions" (PhD dissertation, Monash University, 1982).

39 We have focused our discussion on the number of cadets graduated from the military academy and then inferred from this changes in the size of the commissioned officer corps. The reason for this is that while we have quite complete information about the number of academy graduates, extremely little is known about the total number of commissioned officers on active or *kekaryaan* (civil service) duty at any one time. According to a 1985 report, the Army aimed to have roughly 2,500 officers. See "Reorganisasi, tapi bukan Rasionalisasi, " *Tempo*, May 4, 1985, pp. 12-15. In a subsequent interview, General Rudini estimated that ABRI needed about nine hundred officers of middle (*perwira menengah*) and senior (*perwira tinggi*) rank, the vast majority of whom would come from the Army. Rudini noted that during this transitional period in the mid-1980s, ABRI was in fact short of middle-ranking officers, and so would have to accelerate promotions. This problem, he explained, would be resolved when regular intake from the military academy was *sudah tertib* (orderly) and the numbers of retirees and incomers would *klop* (match). See "Dwifungsi setelah Reorganisasi, " *Tempo*, May 11, 1985, p. 13.

40 See The Editors, "The Indonesian Military in the Mid-1990s: Political Maneuvering or Structural Change?, " *Indonesia* 63 (April 1997): 95. This explanation might account for changes in cadet intake in 1963-65, during the course of *Konfrontasi*, but cannot explain the ongoing increases and decreases over the next decade and a half.

41 Ian MacFarling, *The Dual Function of the Indonesian Armed Forces: Military Politics in Indonesia* (Sydney: Australian Defence Studies Centre, 1996), pp. 146-147. If this was a specific rationale for what can only be termed "over-recruitment, " as MacFarling suggests, one wonders why ABRI never acknowledged it publicly.

Another possible explanation is that annual cadet admissions were decided by the governor of the military academy, and hence that these year-by-year changes reflect different governors' understandings or visions of the Army's personnel needs. But fluctuations in the size of AMN classes in fact do not correspond to the commands of individual governors. During the 1960s graduating class size rose sharply, decreased by half, and then in 1968 increased again to its highest level ever. But one officer, Colonel (later General) Soerono was Governor of the AMN from 1960 until 1966, the period during which these decisions about cadet intake were made.[42] Similarly, during the 1971-1974 period, during which we see cadet intake drop in uneven steps from over four hundred to just one hundred, the academy was governed by the same officer, General Sarwo Edie Wibowo.[43]

Throughout the history of the military academy, decisions about cadet admissions were made by high-ranking staff officers in the respective service branches. According to General (Ret.) Sudiman Saleh, who served as Deputy Governor and Governor of the military academy during the 1980s, there are two sets of considerations involved in the annual decision-making process. First, the Assistant for Personnel (*Aspers Kasum*) estimates the number of officers needed by the Army and evaluates the candidates to determine how many meet the Army's admission requirements. The small numbers of cadets in the early graduating classes were due, at least in part, to the small pool of qualified applicants. This pattern also reflected estimates of future personnel needs. The second part of the process was for the Assistant for Planning (*Asrenum*) to make budget calculations involving the costs of training cadets and supporting the commissioned officer corps. But personnel and budgetary considerations could —and often did —conflict. According to General Sudiman:

> If the budget was short, then the number of cadets would have to be adjusted accordingly. And budget shortfalls were common.

---

42 It is, of course, necessary to make a three-year adjustment to match the date of admission with the graduation date.

43 See Appendix 1.6. The AMN/Akmil Governors were: Soerono (1960-1966), Tahir (1967-1968), Solichin GP (1970), Sarwo Edie (1971-1974), Wiyogo (1975-1977), and Wibisono Gunawan (1978-1980).

Because of that, the total number of cadets accepted didn't always match the personnel projections calculated by the Assistant for Personnel. During the selection process this number might be further reduced because the applicants were not really qualified.[44]

Once settled, however, the intake figures were forwarded to the Army chief of staff and the ABRI commander-in-chief for final approval.

While personnel and budgetary considerations may have guided decisions about cadet intake, there were other factors at work as well. Changing cadet intake and class size must also be understood within the context of developing a modern military academy. Early increases in class size at the AMN during the early and mid 1960s reflected the consolidation of the Army's educational system.[45] When the AMN opened in 1957, it was not the only military academy in Indonesia. At the time, the Academy for Military Technology in Bandung (*Akmil Jurtek*), a training ground for Army engineers and technical specialists, continued to operate. During the early 1960s, the Army's technical educational programs gradually were moved from Akmil Jurtek in Bandung to the AMN in Magelang, thus adding 120 cadets to the AMN class total. These additional specializations appear on the AMN graduation rolls between 1964 and 1966.

Developments at the military academy were not confined to institutional consolidation. When the AMN first opened, educational specialization was limited to four expressly combat courses: Infantry, Cavalry, Artillery, and Anti-aircraft (see Table 1.2). In 1962, along with the addition of the first course from the Akmil Jurtek Bandung, the AMN added a series of further course specializations —Military Police, Transport, Inspection, Health, Adjutant General, Finance, and Law —with the first batch of students in these specialties graduating in 1964. But if this expansion of the military curriculum and total number of cadets was initially part of General Nasution's effort to professionalize the military, it also undoubtedly squared well with the Army's ongoing power struggle with Sukarno and the PKI. Specialization and professional skills would be

---

44 Interview with Sudiman Saleh, Yogyakarta, August 16, 1998.
45 On the proliferation of Army educational centers during the 1950s, see McVey, "The Post-revolutionary Transformation of the Indonesian Army, " Part II, pp. 167-168.

necessary for the military's expansion into the state and the economy. The first sharp increase in the number of graduates from the AMN was the result of the induction of cadets into newly established specializations.

Table 1.2: Cadets Graduated from the National Military Academy by Service Specialization

		Year											
		60	61	62	63	64	65	66	67	68	69	70	71
Specialization	Infantry	13	41	49	80	84	225	165	153	331	-	318	163
	Cavalry	22	51	26	10	12	25	19	15	18	-	19	28
	Field Artillery	9	30	17	12	7	13	9	15	18	-	20	28
	Anti-aircraft	9	29	20	11	10	13	10	20	18	-	19	28
	Communication	-	-	-	-	39	15	15	-	40	-	20	28
	Military Police	-	-	-	-	15	27	7	-	-	-	-	-
	Transport	-	-	-	-	20	30	-	-	-	-	-	-
	Inspection	-	-	-	-	30	20	-	-	-	-	-	-
	Health	-	-	-	-	10	-	-	-	-	-	-	-
	Adjutants	-	-	-	-	25	25	-	-	-	-	-	7
	Finance	-	-	-	-	18	40	-	-	-	-	-	-
	Law	-	-	-	-	10	-	-	-	-	-	-	-
	Engineering	-	-	-	-	-	-	18	-	20	-	41	47
	Equipment	-	-	-	-	-	-	-	-	20	-	-	-
	Topography	-	-	-	-	-	-	-	-	-	-	-	-
Total		53	151	112	113	280	433	243	203	465	-	437	329

Table 1.2 (Continue): Cadets Graduated from the National Military Academy by Service Specialization

	Year												
Specialization	72	73	74	75	76	77	78	79	80	81	82	83	84
Infantry	250	201	203	110	45	20	24	-	43	86	65	128	121
Cavalry	15	19	20	14	-	9	9	-	4	6	4	18	16
Field Artillery	17	16	34a	10	-	7	11	-	4	14	4	13	18
Anti-aircraft	20	-	-	13	-	-	10	-	-	-	4	6	10
Communication	34	38	20	14	9	-	8	-	6	6	4	8	13
Military Police	-	20	31	16	10	9	-	-	5	8	-	-	13
Transport	-	17	32	22	-	5	-	-	5	6	-	-	11
Inspection	-	18	17	22	-	9	-	-	6	8	-	-	13
Health	-	-	-	-	-	-	-	-	-	-	-	-	-
Adjutants	15	15	15	25	-	5	10	-	5	1	-	-	-
Finance	-	15	17	23	-	6	-	-	7	-	-	-	-
Law	-	-	-	-	-	-	-	-	-	-	-	-	-
Engineering	38	40	23	15	8	9	13b	-	11	12	4	11	20
Equipment	-	37	22	14	8	-	8	-	6	7	-	-	9
Topography	-	-	-	6	5	-	-	-	-	-	-	-	-
Total	389	436	434	304	85	79	93	-	102	154	85	184	244

a Includes Anti-aircraft Artillery (Arhanud)

b Includes Topography

Source: *Daftar Alumni AKademi Militer 1948-1996*

The increase in class size during the 1960s resulted not only from the addition of these new specializations, but also from practical considerations that changed over time. Despite the importance General Nasution accorded the re-establishment of the AMN, limited financial resources for constructing the Magelang campus and purchasing training materials, as well as a lack of qualified staff, most likely forced the Army to restrict the size of the early AMN classes.[46] In this light, the subsequent

46 On the importance Nasution attached to the AMN and the ongoing dilemma having to do with resources, see ibid., pp. 162-3, 168.

increase in cadet intake should be viewed as the fulfillment of an initial vision of what the AMN should be and of desired class size rather than as the result of a sudden change in policy.[47]

The seven-fold increase in class size during the first six years of the AMN imparted a particular (and quite significant) stamp on the character of the Army officer corps. Because of both the quality of education offered and the prestige attached to the AMN, the early graduates enjoyed an advantage (though the extent of this is debatable) over older, less educated officers as well as over graduates of the other military educational institutions. And, as we will argue in a later section, the high level of career success enjoyed by the relatively small graduating classes from the AMN in the early 1960s surely influenced the career expectations of the later, but far larger, classes which graduated during the late 1960s and first half of the 1970s.

Far more difficult to explain is the sudden and precipitous reduction of about 75 percent in the number of cadets graduating from Akabri beginning in 1975-76.[48] No official explanation for this can be found in the literature. The only professional rationale for such a change would be to accommodate a corresponding decrease in the size of the Army as a whole. But this did not occur. Nor is it likely that the Army's budget was slashed suddenly by 75 percent, necessitating drastic cuts in cadet acceptance.[49] Although the timing appears wrong, Jenkins offers one plausible explanation: "[b]y 1980, it had become clear that the Military Academy (Akabri) at Magelang was not attracting the cream of the nation's youth, the obvious possibilities for self-advancement in the military sphere notwithstanding."[50] This being the case, it is possible that members of the military elite decided that it was more important to maintain high standards, even if this required reducing class size, than it was to maintain the current size of the commissioned officer corps.

---

47 This line of argument still does not account for the sharp decrease in the size of AMN Class 8 (1967) and Class 9 (1968).

48 The absence of a graduating class in 1979 was the result of a shift in the start of the academic year nation-wide. We are grateful to Nobertus Nuranto for bringing this to our attention.

49 In 1973-74, at the time these classes were inducted into the military academy, Indonesia was experiencing huge trade surpluses as a result of the rise in world oil prices.

50 Jenkins, *Suharto and His Generals*, pp. 258-259. This view is supported by General Sudiman, according to whom there was a serious difficulty in finding "quality human resources." Interview, August 16, 1998.

Another possible explanation is that this marked change in Akabri output is related to the establishment of the Officer Candidate School (Sekolah Calon Perwira; Secapa) in Bandung or a new policy allowing Secapa graduates to compete with Akabri officers for middle-ranking (*perwira menengah*) staff and command positions.[51]

Here, it is instructive to consider the changes in service specialization. The initial drop in class size coming in 1975 is reflected entirely in the number of infantry cadets, the number of cadets in the other specialties remaining unchanged. In 1976, however, this was followed by an across-the-board reduction in the number of cadets trained in each service specialization, as well as a temporary suspension of a number of these courses. Remarkably, when these classes reached middle-level ranks they would not have a sufficient number of field officers to staff all Kodim commands.[52]

Finally, beginning in 1984, Akabri class size stabilized at around 250 cadets per year and remained at this level throughout the decade.[53] Although we do not know how many officers the Army actually requires to fill all middle- and senior-level staff and command positions, something on the order of two hundred to three hundred new officers per year would seem to be a reasonable number.[54]

RUN-UP TO THE 1997 ELECTIONS

Over the past several years, members of the Indonesian military elite have intimated that there are problems with the promotional process and

---

51 Little information is available about Secapa, but it appears that this program only began in 1990/1991, with 352 cadets in the first class. See "KSAD: Calon Perwira harus Jauhkan Ambisi Pribadinya, " *Kompas*, December 21, 1992.

52 Assuming a standard two-year tour of duty for middle-ranking officers, and recalling the total number of Kodim in Indonesia, each class from the military academy would need 140 field officers to fill these positions alone. However, Class 16 (1976) produced a mere forty-five field officers (all infantry), Class 17 (1977) only thrity-six (infantry, cavalry, and field artillery combined), and so on. These large deficits will have to be made up either through the assignment of greater numbers of Secapa graduates or by extending the tour of duty for military academy graduates. Members of these small classes are currently being assigned to Kodim commands.

53 In light of the 1983-1985 reorganization of the military, this new level was likely set by ABRI Commander-in-Chief General Moerdani and Army Chief of Staff General Rudini.

54 Furthermore, it should be recalled that graduates of Secapa are allowed to compete with Akabri graduates for at least some middle-level positions (e.g. Kodim commander), thus adding to the overall size of the commissioned officer corps.

placement of officers within both the Army and the Armed Forces high command. In March 1996, the magazine *Forum Keadilan* titled a special feature "When there is a Promotional Log-jam at the Top." The feature discussed the institutional dilemma that took place "when, for the first time ever, two lieutenant generals are entitled to be promoted to the same position" and goes on to note that two other active lieutenant generals were still awaiting assignment because no posts of the appropriate rank were vacant.[55]

Major General Theo Syafei, an outspoken member of the ABRI faction of the People's Representative Council (F-ABRI DPR-RI) labeled the problem "General Inflation," attributing it to the policy of assigning posts within the Armed Forces on the basis of military rank. Syafei's comments initiated a highly revealing debate over the current system and procedures for transfers and promotions. Tati Darsoyo, another member of the People's Representative Council, posed questions about the root of the dilemma: "Is this [issue of assignments] wrong and problematic because we assign positions and posts in accordance with rank or because of some other reason?"[56] Similarly, the usually staid Minister of Security General Edi Sudradjat asked flatly: "Are rotations taking place too quickly?" In answer to his own question, Edi noted that the military as an institution would settle the matter, a clear reference to maintaining military autonomy in the face of personal or palace preference.[57]

The May 1997 national legislative elections were to have a significant impact on this promotional log-jam within the Army officer corps. This is worth considering in some detail. As early as November 1995 military leaders announced that the ongoing waves of personnel rotations were in preparation for the May 1997 elections, a full one and a half years away.[58] Several months later, following an additional wave of personnel changes, members of the military elite made increasingly frequent statements that further transfers would not take place until after the 1997 parliamentary elections. In February 1996, ABRI Commander-in-Chief General

---

55 "Bila Gerbang Mutas Macet di Atas, " *Forum Keadilan*, March 25, 1996, pp. 12-14. The article overstates its case: this was a common occurrence during the 1950s and early 1960s.
56 Ibid., p. 12.
57 Quoted in "Pangab Mengenai Tiga Letjen tak Punya Jabatan, " *Kompas*, March 6, 1996.
58 "Peluang Lulusan AMN Kian Mengecil: Mutasi di Tubuh ABRI Berkaitan dengan Pemilu, " *Merdeka*, November 20, 1995.

Feisal Tanjung announced that "in principle" there would be no further transfers until after the 1997 elections, but that if any did take place they would be "few in number and most likely not involve field commanders but rather staff positions."[59] In reference to the politically sensitive Kodam commands, General Feisal Tanjung commented that "the corps of Kodam commanders remains solid,"[60] noting specifically that "the Commander of Kodam Jaya (Jakarta), Major General Wiranto, will continue to hold his position until the 1997 election."[61] If implemented, this pre-election policy would effectively have served to exacerbate the existing promotional backlog within the Army elite, thus holding back the careers of hundreds of middle-ranking officers. This also means that we should have seen an increase in the mean tenure of commanding officers. It was on the basis of these official statements that Harold Crouch and other observers argued that the most recent waves of transfers were intended to ensure "a similarity of political vision in the military in facing the 1997 elections."[62]

Yet official statements proved to be misleading at best. A mere one month later, in mid-March 1996, an additional wave of personnel rotations was announced involving senior officers in the Armed Forces and Army high commands. These rotations included the strategic appointments of Lieutenant General Wiranto as Kostrad commander, his replacement as Kodam Jaya (Jakarta) commander by Major General Sutiyoso, and the appointment of the rising star Major General Bambang Yudhoyono as Chief of Staff Kodam Jaya (Jakarta).[63]

These personnel transfers were followed by a curious series of statements by senior military brass. In May 1996, Army Chief of Staff General R. Hartono announced that "in addition to organizational requirements, the change of Kodam commanders is related to the upcoming 1997 election." Hartono added, however, that while he could make suggestions about needed personnel changes, the final decisions

---

59 "Pangab: Prinsipnya, Sampai Pemilu tak Ada Lagi Mutasi, " *Kompas*, February 17, 1996.

60 "Pangab: Barisan Pangdam Masih Solid, " *Merdeka*, February 17, 1996.

61 "Hingga Pemilu tidak ada Pergantian Pangdam, " *Media Indonesia*, February 17, 1996.

62 See, for example, the interview with Harold Crouch, "Crouch: ABRI Rapatkan Barisan, " *Merdeka*, February 24, 1996, and "Dr. A. Yahya Muhaimin: Pergantian Pimpinan ABRI Mengantisipasi Pemilu 1997, " *Kompas*, March 11, 1996.

63 See, for example, "Empat Mutasi di tubuh ABRI dalam 50 Hari, " *Republika*, March 18, 1996.

lay with ABRI Commander-in-Chief Feisal Tanjung.[64] Given that Feisal
had repeatedly stated that there would be no further rotations prior to
the May 1997 election, these comments appear more as a challenge to
than acknowledgment of the Commander-in-Chief's authority. In June,
ABRI Chief of Staff for General Affairs Lieutenant General Soeyono
added a further note, warning that if members of AMN Class 10 (1970)
were not appointed to senior positions by 1997, that "our regeneration
will be late and [the officers] will be slow to mature."[65] Again, in obvious
contradiction to the numerous statements made by ABRI Commander-
in-Chief Feisal Tanjung, Soeyono argued publicly that the tenure of the
current Kodam commanders should not be extended simply because of
the 1997 election.

Indeed, despite the flurry of official statements about pre-election
promotional policy, yet another wave of personnel changes was announced
in August 1996. This, the fourth major personnel shift of the year,
included the replacement of three Kodam commanders.[66] These moves
were followed in September by a fifth reshuffling, this involving another
one hundred senior officers.[57] Despite official statements to the contrary,
personnel changes were not only continuing, but in fact intensifying.

How then are we to interpret Feisal Tanjung's repeated claims that
transfers would be held off until after the election? The seriousness with
which ABRI prepared for the 1997 elections cannot be doubted. Senior
military officials made almost daily statements about the necessity of
"safeguarding" the election. They offered warnings that ABRI would not
tolerate disruption of the electoral process. The military daily *Angkatan
Bersenjata* commonly reported on the training of special troops (complete
with riot gear) to prevent unrest during the election period. But these
moves do not adequately explain the ongoing personnel changes, nor the
apparent inconsistencies between official statements denying that further
personnel changes would take place and the ongoing appointment of new
Kodam commanders.

---

64 "Pergantian Pejabat TNI AD Berkait dengan Pemilu, " *Kompas*, May 27, 1996.
65 "Perwira angkatan 70 harus berperan sesudah Pemilu nanti, " *Angkatan Bersenjata*, June 16, 1996.
66 "Pergantian di ABRI: Dari Angkatan '65 ke Angkatan '65", *Republika*, August 12, 1996.
67 See "Jabatan Assospol Kassospol serta Danpussenif diserahterimakan, " *Angkatan Bersenjata*, September 23, 1996, and "70 Pati ABRI alih jabatan, " *Angkatan Bersenjata*, September 24, 1996.

One alternative view, building on previous analyses by the editors of *Indonesia*, is that the March and August waves of personnel changes represented "Palace-inspired countermeasures" pushed through against the will of senior military leaders.[68] In this regard, the assignment of Major General Wiranto to the strategic post of Kostrad commander and his replacement as commander of Kodam Jaya (Jakarta) by Major General Sutiyoso would appear to have strengthened Presidential security. But while this line of argument can account for the appointment of a few individuals in and around Jakarta, it cannot explain the necessity for increasingly rapid personnel changes throughout the Army and across the archipelago.

Another possible explanation, and the one that we propose, is that despite an official desire to maintain the current command line-up at the time, continued personnel rotations were necessary in order to prevent a worsening of the promotional log-jam. This was true not only at the pinnacle of the officer corps, but also among the middle-ranking officers who oversee the daily operation of the territorial security system. This is not to deny that the President might have benefited from these changes as well (though recent events reveal that he did not!). In other words, the necessity of maintaining institutional rationality through the continued transfer and promotion of Army officers might have forced the hand of the military elite in a way that in fact coincided with President Soeharto's interests. The rapid rotation of Kodam and Korem commanders limited the possibility of an officer developing a regional "interest" or personal influence over combat troops. And the ongoing transfers allowed the President to appoint a core group of officers in and around the capital who not only shared similar interests, but whose interests largely coincided with those of the President himself.

Elsewhere, however, further rotations and promotions were in fact held off or disguised because of the election. Rotation and replacement of Korem commanders throughout Indonesia was put on hold for six months prior to the May election.[69] The delay in replacing Korem

---

68 The Editors, "Current Data on the Indonesian Military Elite: January 1, 1992 - August 31, 1993, " *Indonesia* 56 (October 1993): 119, 123.

69 The last changes of Korem commanders prior to the May election took place in October 1996, involving the commanders of Korem 044 Garuda Dempo (South Sumatra) and Korem 091 Aji

commanders caused by the election was further attested to by the flurry of personnel changes in the month after the election. In many respects, however, these changes were also misleading. Following a tour of duty as Korem commander, officers with the rank of colonel who are slated for further promotion normally attend the nine-month course at the National Defense Institute (Lemhanas) in Jakarta, which begins in early April. While the military wished to forestall personnel changes, it could not put career advancement on hold, and a number of these officers moved to Jakarta in April while still formally in command of regional Korem.[70] This dilemma of timing and the Army's response provides insight into the strategic thinking of the Army elite. First, the appointment of new Korem commanders immediately prior to the election would leave these territorial units in the hands of officers who had not had time to establish a broad network of social contacts. Second, the decision to leave Korem units under the command of officers who were not in fact present in the field opened the possibility that military responses to disorder or security challenges might be delayed, or that poor decisions might be made by inexperienced subordinates. And third, public knowledge of personnel changes at the time of the election might encourage more open challenges to local authorities.

Further rotations and reassignments were also deferred until after the election to determine which officers would be assigned *kekaryaan* posts as members of national and local legislatures. In early July, it was announced that five Kodam commanders would be made members of the national parliament (DPR-RI) and replaced shortly.[71] More massive rotations

---

Surya Natakusuma (East Kalimantan). At the time, neither of the incumbents had served for long (twelve and twenty-one months respectively), and these replacements may reflect concern about the historic strength of the United Development Party (PPP) in South Sumatra and the Indonesian Democratic Party (PDI) in East Kalimantan.

70 Officers who moved to Jakarta in early April included Colonel Ferrial Sofyan, commander of Korem 041 (Bengkulu) and Colonel Bachtiar Lutfi Sjukri, commander of Korem 101 (South Kalimantan), where major election-related violence occurred. These transfers are discussed in "Korem Gamas harus tingkatkan komitmen pengabdian," *Angkatan Bersenjata*, June 10, 1997, and "Sertijab Danrem 101 tidak ada kaitan dengan kerusuhan," *Angkatan Bersenjata*, June 4, 1997. It is not known when Colonel Achmad Yahya, Korem 131 (North Sulawesi), Colonel Iping Sumantri, Korem 162 (West Nusatenggara), and Colonel Mahidin Simbolon, Korem 164 (East Timor) left their posts for Lemhanas. See "Pangdam Udayana Nilai NTB Rawan," *Jawa Pos*, June 22, 1997, and "Serah Terima Jabatan Tiga Komandan Korem," *Kompas*, June 1, 1997.

71 "Syarwan Masuk DPR Bersama Lima Pangdam," *Kompas*, July 10, 1997.

subsequently took place at the Kodim level, resulting in the replacement of almost all officers who graduated from the military academy prior to 1974. These moves left the local level military apparatus in the hands of the far smaller Akmil classes of the late 1970s and early 1980s, the professional and political attitudes of whom remain largely unknown.

CONCLUSIONS

While professional militaries are premised on stability and regularity, during the 1990s personnel changes within the Indonesian Army took place with increasing frequency and scope. We have argued that appeals to individual personalities, attempts to assuage military-Islamic relations, and concerns about "safeguarding" the 1997 election do not adequately account for these changes. Rather, the increasingly frequent personnel changes among the Indonesian military elite during the 1990s are best understood as a function of the changing size of the Army officer corps. But while the rapidity of personnel rotations and promotions is a clear response to the swollen size of the officer corps, the reduced size of Akmil classes beginning in 1976 should lead to a corresponding slow-down in personnel changes as these classes reach middle ranks. Coupled with the flurry of post-election personnel reshuffles, this would suggest an increase in command tenure for at least middle-ranking officers in the future.

CHAPTER TWO
CAREER PATTERNS IN THE INDONESIAN ARMY

There is perhaps nothing more problematic for a modern military than for decisions regarding the assignment and promotion of officers to be made based on political or personal considerations. To do so seriously undermines respect within the officer corps for professional norms and strains the chain of command. Over the past decade, observers of the Indonesian Army have often noted the capricious nature of the assignment and promotional process and the central role of *koneksi* (connections). In a 1993 update, the editors of the journal *Indonesia* argued that President Soeharto increasingly "had to rely on the promotion and appointment to key positions of relatives, former personal adjutants, and members of ethnic minorities, in order to maintain his grip."[1] There can be no doubt that this is true.

Examples of political and personal considerations in assignment and promotion are both numerous and well-publicized in the Indonesian media. Prominent relatives who have enjoyed senior appointments in the Armed Forces include presidential brother-in-law Wismoyo Arismunandar, who served as Army Chief of Staff from 1993 to 1995, and presidential son-in-law Prabowo S. Djojohadikusumo, who rose to his position as Commander of the Army Strategic Command (Kostrad) in near-record time. Officers who served the President personally have also benefited handsomely from their contacts and presumed loyalty. After serving as Presidential Adjutant for four years, General Wiranto was rapidly promoted to command Kodam Jaya (the Greater Jakarta

---

1 The Editors, "Current Data on the Indonesian Military Elite: January 1, 1992-August 31, 1993, " *Indonesia* 56 (October 1993): 123.

Regional Military Command), to become commander of Kostrad, and then in 1997 he became Army Chief of Staff, with the rank of four-star general. In 1998, following the selection of Soeharto to an ill-fated seventh term as President, Wiranto was appointed as ABRI Commander-in-Chief and simultaneously as Minister of Defense. Major General Soegiono, who was selected to replace Wiranto in the strategic position of Kostrad commander, had also previously served as Presidential Adjutant and as commander of the Presidential Guard (*Pasukan Pengawal Presiden*).

These and other cases have had a major influence on the analysis of Indonesian military politics during the 1990s. This is as much because the officers involved are readily identifiable as it is because the practices they reveal are of tremendous concern within the officer corps. In a think-tank report that circulated on the Internet in early 1997, the politicization of the assignment and promotional process was highlighted as one of the central points of conflict within the military. The report attempts to paint General Wiranto as a hypocrite:

> Wiranto presents an image of himself as a professional soldier who is disgusted by the politicking raging within ABRI. His close friends tell stories that Wiranto often complains that rotations and promotions within ABRI are motivated by political calculations based on what is referred to as the "Prabowo-Hartono-Ms. Tutut Network."[2]

Unstated, but all too well known in Indonesia, is the fact that Wiranto himself served as Presidential Adjutant for four years and was commonly rumored to be the officer most trusted by President Soeharto. The problem of *koneksi* may indeed be of serious concern to senior military officers, particularly for those who wish to maintain the military's autonomy and bureaucratic norms and to resist presidential control over

---

2   Major General Prabowo is a Presidential son-in-law; Lieutenant General Hartono was the Army Chief of Staff until mid-1997; Ms. Tutut is the nickname of the President's eldest daughter, Siti Hardijanti Rukmana. Quoted in "Analisis Perkembangan Sosial-Politik Menjelang Pemilu 1997 dan SU-MPR 1998, " posted on <APAKABAR@clark.net>; reportedly written by members of the Centre for Policy Development Studies (CPDS), and circulated on the Internet. This report is attributed to a team consisting of Dr. Amir Santoso, Dr. Dien Sjamsuddin, Major General Muchlis Anwar, Lukman Harun, and Brigadier General Robik Mukav.

the Armed Forces. But given the large size of the commissioned officer corps, personal and political considerations can play a role in no more than a tiny percentage of the total number of all appointments. The vast majority of officers are neither related to the first family nor have served the President in a direct capacity.

Ironically, this analytical focus on the politicization of personnel decisions at the top of the Indonesian Armed Forces is frequently complemented by a seemingly contradictory position. Among observers of the Indonesian military there is an assumption that the Army and Armed Forces headquarters have some sort of promotional master plan. To cite but one example, Lowry writes that "[a] systematic, if not impartial, posting and rotation system has been instituted in the officer corps which has played an important role in limiting the chances of individual senior or charismatic officers developing personal followings."[3] According to this line of thought there is (or should be) a clear and specific reason for the assignment and promotion of each and every officer. These reasons may have to do with institutional needs of the military or the experiences and skills of individual officers. In either case it is assumed that particular officers are carefully chosen for each posting for specific reasons.

There is, however, reason to believe that this notion suggesting the existence of a master plan may well exaggerate the extent of personnel planning within the Armed Forces. Army records are probably not as good as is commonly assumed. In August 1997, for example, the Army Adjutant-General, Brigadier General M. Y. Indung Hariyanto, made a public statement about the need to improve the dossiers kept on Army officers in order to facilitate transfers and assignments, promotions in rank, and the issuing of service rewards and medals.[4] Indeed, over the past decade, the armed forces newspaper, *Angkatan Bersenjata*, has carried remarkably few references to personnel files and record-keeping, suggesting that this issue has received little attention within the military.

---

3 Robert Lowry, *The Armed Forces of Indonesia* (St. Leonards: Allen & Unwin, 1996), p. 65. As if to deny his own argument, several pages later Lowry concludes: "Much of ABRI's centralization and unity of command depends on the ability of one man, President Suharto, to manipulate the promotion and posting of officers..." (p. 85).

4 See "Dosir pelancar dibirokratisasi pembinaan prajurit TNI-AD, " *Angkatan Bersenjata*, August 2, 1997.

We are thus left with a picture of the assignment process for Army officers in which there is little middle ground between the extremes of personal *koneksi* and a vague but overriding institutional logic. This chapter will argue that appeals to *koneksi* and institutional logic can only offer partial explanations of the complex assignment process for commissioned officers. This raises several fundamental questions: On what basis are assignments and promotions decided? What determines career success of commissioned Army officers? What assignments are most likely to lead to further promotions and the rise to senior ranks? To answer these questions, ideally one would like to be able to analyze a host of variables together: ethnicity, religion, class rank at the military academy, service specialization, personal connections, combat experience, previous posts held, the effect of one's cohort on individual success, and so forth. With complete data, we could thoroughly analyze these variables for the 4,500 officers who graduated from the military academy during the 1960s and the first half of the 1970s to determine the relative importance of each of these factors.

Since this is impossible due to a lack of data, this chapter will adopt a phenomenological approach to promotional practice, examining the prerogative left to commanding officers, recommendations made by outgoing officers, precedent, and the effect of each cohort of graduates from the military academy on more junior classes. We will argue that each of these factors, although rarely noted, is of central importance in the assignment and promotion process and, by extension, in determining career success. Furthermore, these findings allow us to refine the previous chapter's argument concerning command tenure. The chapter then turns to a broader examination of career paths within the Indonesian Army. The identification of assignment and promotional patterns within the Army provides insight into the expectations and performance of Army officers.

THE ROLE OF RECOMMENDATIONS AND CLASS SOLIDARITY

Unfortunately we know all too little about either the official policy or practice of assignments and promotions. In theory, all personnel decisions are made or approved by one of the ABRI Boards for Assignments and

Rank.[5] In practice, however, it appears that these boards are largely limited to decisions regarding officers of general rank and, to a lesser degree, the assignment of middle-ranking officers (colonels in particular) to strategic positions. These senior appointments, of course, are precisely the domain in which presidential whim and other forms of politicking are most common and carry the greatest weight. Below the rank of general, however, the assignment and promotion processes operate quite differently. In the territorial units, it is the duty of the Assistant for Personnel to forward personnel recommendations to his commanding officer (be it a Kodim, Korem, or Kodam commander), who reviews these recommendations and forwards them to Army headquarters for approval.

It is worth asking whether, as is the case with commanding officers (see chapter one), the tenure of Assistants for Personnel has decreased. If these officers serve significantly longer than their colleagues in other comparable posts, this would suggest that the greater stability of these positions results from a conscious decision on the part of the military to guarantee proper oversight of personnel decisions. If, however, tenure in these posts is as short (or shorter) than that for commanders, it would indicate that little thought is being given to the promotional process in the territorial commands. The available data show that tenure trends for personnel officers have declined along with the trends for commanding officers of similar rank, suggesting that those making personnel decisions are doing so with less knowledge of the officer corps in their territorial unit than was the case with their predecessors. During the 1990s a surprisingly large number of these officers were transferred from one Kodam to serve as either the Deputy Assistant or Assistant for Personnel in another Kodam where they lacked previous experience. These features suggest that the officers involved do not have significant knowledge either of the local needs or of the members of the officer corps, and may also indicate

---

5 There are separate boards for junior and senior officers, *Dewan Jabatan dan Kepangkatan Perwira ABRI* and *Dewan Jabatan dan Kepangkatan Perwira Tinggi ABRI* (Wanjakti), respectively. Additionally, there are unique procedures regarding assignment to *kekaryaan* duty. Both Armed Forces Headquarters and Regional Military Commanders may nominate an officer as a candidate for an administrative post. Officers who wish to be considered for a position as *Bupati* or *Walikota* may also request permission from ABRI headquarters to be listed as candidates. One of the few discussions of this is found in "Saifullah: Belum Dapat Restu dari Mabes ABRI, " *Pikiran Rakyat*, November 22, 1997.

that there is in fact no "master plan" regarding personnel decisions.

In addition to standard recommendations made by the Board for Assignments and Rank and Assistants for Personnel at the various territorial commands, a certain degree of discretion regarding assignments is left to the commanders of territorial and combat units. This is particularly true when a new commander is installed, for he "is supposed to have the authority to set up his own chain of command."[6] Even after this initial period, a Kodam or Korem commander may enter a request for a particular officer to be assigned (or reassigned to a new post) under his command. Such requests and recommendations made by local and regional commanders are not always fulfilled, however. The recent choice of a new commander of the politically strategic Korem 084 Surabaya is illustrative. The *Surabaya Post* reported that the commander of Kodam V Brawijaya (East Java), Major General Imam Oetomo, recommended that one of his assistants be chosen to fill the opening as Korem 084 commander. This input was ignored by superiors in Army headquarters, and a relatively obscure officer who had previously served at the Army Staff and Command School in Bandung was selected instead.[7]

Recommendations regarding assignments are not limited to commanding officers. According to the editors of the journal *Indonesia*, an officer being transferred from a post in which he has completed a tour of duty is normally allowed to recommend a suitable replacement for the post he is vacating. Given the high level of solidarity among classmates at the military academy, it is common for out-going officers to recommend that a classmate fill the vacancy. The editors of *Indonesia* note this practice in passing as one important explanation for the overall "success" of particular cohorts from the academy: the star members of a class recommend and thereby further the careers of their classmates for assignment to particular posts.[8]

It is clear that among the higher ranks, Army officers have definite opinions about who is suited to fill their position. Upon being informed

---

6 The Editors, "Current Data on the Indonesian Military Elite: January 1, 1992-August 31, 1993, " p. 123.

7 Discussed in "Kol. Bambang Satriawan Calon Danrem Surabaya, " *Surabaya Post*, September 4, 1997.

8 The Editors, "Current Data on the Indonesian Military Elite: January 1, 1992-April 3, 1993, " *Indonesia* 55 (April 1993): 180.

of rumors that Brigadier General Johnny Lumintang was slated to become commander of Kodam VIII Trikora (Irian Jaya province), outgoing Kodam VIII commander Major General Dunidja commented: "So there's continuity. I think that's fine."[9] Not only had Lumintang served as Chief of Staff of Kodam VIII under Dunidja's command, but he had succeeded Dunidja in several previous postings.[10] But without access to Army policy manuals or confirmation from officers knowledgeable about the assignment process, it is difficult to evaluate the weight carried by recommendations made by outgoing commanders in general or those by classmates in particular.

Even so, we might address the issue by adopting a phenomenological approach. We can begin by forming an initial hypothesis: the maintenance of institutional rationality — what the Army now commonly refers to as ensuring that *regenerasi* (regeneration) continues on schedule — should mean that an outgoing officer will normally be replaced by an officer from a more junior class from the military academy. This might be specified further in relation to the Army's standard tour of duty: given a hypothetical two-year tour of duty,[11] officers selected for a position should be two classes junior to the outgoing officer. This would ensure that the holder of a particular post will always be of roughly the same age and that (given an equal division of appointments at the outset) each class will receive approximately equal numbers of assignments to each type of post.

While it is theoretically possible to carry out such an analysis for all positions within the Army, it will be simpler (and perhaps more valuable) to limit our sample to several key command positions. The data for a sample of Kodam and Korem commanders are shown in Table 2.1. The column labeled "AMN Class difference" refers to the number of years difference in graduating class from the military academy between

---

9   His words: "Jadi nyambung. Saya kira bagus." Quoted in "Pangdam: Tiga Pangdam Baru, " *Gatra*, August 10, 1996.

10 Lumintang succeeded Dunidja as Commander of the Core Infantry Regiment in Kodam Jaya (Jakarta), followed him in the high-profile position of commander of Korem 164 Wira Dharma (East Timor), and was then assigned as Dunidja's Chief of Staff in Kodam VIII (Irian Jaya).

11 Although members of the military elite have intimated that three years is the desired norm, based on the tenure trends presented in chapter one we suggest using a hypothetical two-year tour of duty.

a newly appointed commander and his predecessor (i.e. -2 means that an officer is two years senior to his predecessor, +2 means that he is two years junior). Contrary to the hypothesized pattern, it is in fact very common for classmates to succeed one another. We find that nearly a quarter (23.3 percent) of all Korem commanders succeeded their classmates from the military academy, and another 28.8 percent were only one class junior. The corresponding figures for Kodam commanders are 28.4 percent and 27.2 percent respectively. In all, the average AMN class difference for Korem commanders is only 1.37 years and that for Kodam commanders 1.16, both far short of the hypothesized two-year difference.

Table 2.1:

Class Difference Between Successive Commanders, 1985-1997
(as a percentage of known universe)

AMN Class Difference	Korem Commanders	Kodam Commanders
-3	-	1.2
-2	0.8	4.9
-1	3.8	4.9
0	23.3	28.4
+1	28.8	27.2
+2	20.8	12.3
+3	18.6	11.1
+4	3.0	4.9
+5	0.8	1.2
+6	-	2.5
+7	-	1.2

The high frequency with which classmates succeed each other as territorial commanders is strong (although still indirect) evidence that recommendations made by outgoing officers do carry weight in the assignment process. Direct evidence would require statements by senior military officers, something that is not available.

As the following section will argue, this practice has also played a contributing role in the promotional log-jam discussed in chapter one and, by extension, added a further twist to the problem of tenure within the Army officer corps.[12]

THE STANDARDIZATION OF OFFICER APPOINTMENTS

The frequency with which classmates from the military academy have succeeded one another in the same posts provides insight into relative class strength. The more successful the members of a particular cohort are at recommending and thereby helping their classmates, the greater will be the overall career success of that cohort. Furthermore, the relative success of one class will affect the prospects for subsequent (junior) classes. Thus, for example, the prominence of AMN Class 2 (1961) and Class 3 (1962) in Korem commands during the late 1980s can be said to have held back the advancement of AMN Class 4 (1963) and Class 5 (1964) to these same posts. Conversely, the relative lack of success of these two classes created openings for their immediate juniors, the members of AMN Class 6 (1965) and AMN Class 7 (1966).

The ballooning size of classes graduating from the military academy during the mid-1960s added a new dimension to this equation. Totaling 433 cadets, Class 6 (1965) was the first of the large cohorts to graduate from the academy. Not only did this class have an exceptionally large number of officers appointed as Korem commanders (fifty-six), but nearly half of these officers were appointed to succeed their own classmates.[13] This, in effect, means that Class 6 (1965) received a "double" allotment of Korem commands. Several years later, when these officers came of rank for more senior assignments, a virtually identical situation emerged with respect to the allotment of Kodam commands. There is no obvious policy reason why this occurred, and indeed bureaucratic norms should have prevented such a stranglehold by one cohort on command positions at a given rank. One possible explanation is that the Army and Armed Forces high commands were simply unaware of or unprepared for this significant increase in AMN class size and failed to take this into account

---

12 The relationship between recommendations, age at the time of appointment to command posts, and tenure of commanding officers is discussed in Appendix 2.1.

13 This figure is based on the forty-seven officers from AMN Class 6 (1965) for whom an immediate successor and his graduating class can be identified.

when making personnel decisions. Another possibility is that there was a shortage of qualified officers at just the time that Class 6 (1965) was reaching middle rank, and that this opened opportunities for an inordinate number of officers from this class to hold the most sought after positions. Still another possible reason is that particular classes from the military academy were aligned with different political interests (e.g. the Palace circle of President Soeharto versus General Benny Moerdani), and thus received preferential treatment.[14] While the precise reasons for this "monopolization" of command posts remain unknown, it is clear that the relative success of different classes from the military academy compounded the existing dilemmas posed by the changing size of the Army officer corps.

The remarkable success of the officers of Class 6 (1965) should, in theory, have had a deleterious effect on the immediately junior Class 7 (1966) and Class 8 (1967). The editors of *Indonesia* addressed just this possibility:

> ...the unusually large Class 6 (1965) held back Class 7 and possibly Class 8 from reaching command positions in Korem in the late 1980s and early 1990s. Now dominant in the army central and regional commands, Class 6 officers again threaten to hold back Class 7, 8, and 9 from reaching staff and command positions in the army central and regional commands.[15]

Indeed, we might suspect that, following its long hold on Korem commands during the late 1980s and early 1990s, the members of Class 6 (1965) would be succeeded by officers several years their junior to remedy the promotional log-jam. This, however, was not the case. Rather, the data reveal that two different "corrections" took place.

The first of these "corrections" involved the total number of officers per class to be appointed as Korem commander. Although the extraordinary success of Class 6 (1965) was followed by a decrease in the number of

---

14 This suggestion is made in The Editors, "Current Data on the Indonesian Military Elite: January 1, 1992-August 31, 1993, " p. 121.

15 The Editors, "Current Data on the Indonesian Military Elite: September 1, 1993-August 31, 1994, " *Indonesia* 58 (October 1994): 86.

Korem commanders given to junior classes, neither of the immediately subsequent classes fared particularly poorly overall: Class 7 (1966) had twenty-one officers appointed as Korem commander, and Class 8 (1967) had twenty-nine. Taken together, Classes 7 to 12 (for which complete data are available) received an average of twenty-two Korem commands each.[16] This is, in fact, extremely close to the outcome that one would have predicted given that there are thirty-nine such commands and assuming a desired tour of duty of two years. What took place, therefore, was a form of standardization: the Army high command apparently learned from the "mistake" of allowing one class to monopolize command positions and since then has allotted roughly equal numbers of these assignments to each cohort from the military academy.[17]

The second "correction" following the monopoly success of Class 6 (1965) concerned mean tenure of Korem commanders. In an early version of this work, we suggested that the military high command had responded to the increased size of the officer corps through two means: first, reducing tenure in order to give more officers a chance to hold coveted command positions; second, instituting a form of job sharing, whereby classmates would succeed one another but for brief terms.[18] The available data now show that this second conclusion was incorrect. Rather than seeing mean tenure decrease for large cohorts and rise for small cohorts, we find that there is in fact no clear correlation between class size and command tenure. Mean tenure for Korem commanders from the very large Class 6 (1965) as a whole was nearly seven hundred days, significantly higher than that for the far smaller Class 7 (1966) and Class 8 (1967) (see Figure 2.1). Even with the subsequent increase in class size during the early 1970s, mean tenure for Korem commanders remained at this reduced level. This same standardization emerges in the data for Kodam commanders, where each class from 1965 on served nearly identical tenures, regardless of overall class size (see Figure 2.2).

---

16 Data on the total number of Korem and Kodam commanders from each class is presented in Table 3.1 in chapter three, following.

17 The implications of this on career prospects will be explored in chapter three.

18 See The Editors, "The Indonesian Military in the Mid-1990s: Political Maneuvering or Structural Change?" *Indonesia* 63 (April 1997): 99.

To these two "corrections" we can add a third form of standardization in the appointment of Army officers. From the time of General Moerdani's reorganization of the Army in 1985 until the present, the variability in length of tenure for Army commanders has decreased markedly (see Figures 2.3 and 2.4). For example, the tenure of Korem commanders who completed their tour of duty in 1987 varied from a low of approximately three hundred days to a high of over 1,600 days. In 1996 and 1997, by contrast, the range of tenure is limited to a much smaller range, between three hundred and nine hundred days. The data are equally dramatic for Kodam commanders. From 1987 until 1993, the period immediately following Moerdani's reorganization of the Army, command tenure varied from a low of two hundred days to a high of over 1,200 days. From 1993 until the present, by contrast, tenure variability has been confined within a far tighter band. This does not necessarily mean that the Army adopted new policies,[19] though this is possible, but merely that there has been a change in the practice regarding tour of duty for commissioned officers.

Significant conclusions follow from these findings. First, the Indonesian Army was largely unprepared for the dramatic increase in the size of graduating classes from the military academy. Failing to compensate for this change when the large Class 6 (1965) made the rank of colonel beginning in the mid-1980s therefore exacerbated the existing structural dilemma posed by larger class size.[20] In other words, the decrease in command tenure during the 1990s was a necessary response to *both* the increased size of the officer corps *and* the monopoly of AMN Class 6 (1965). The second point follows from the first: the Army elite learned from these experiences by implementing a number of "corrective" measures to normalize the assignment process.

---

19 See chapter one, footnote 6 for details.
20 It should be noted that this effect only appears at the rank of colonel and above; the decrease in tenure among battalion and Kodim commanders during the 1990s can be accounted for solely in relation to the changing size of the officer corps.

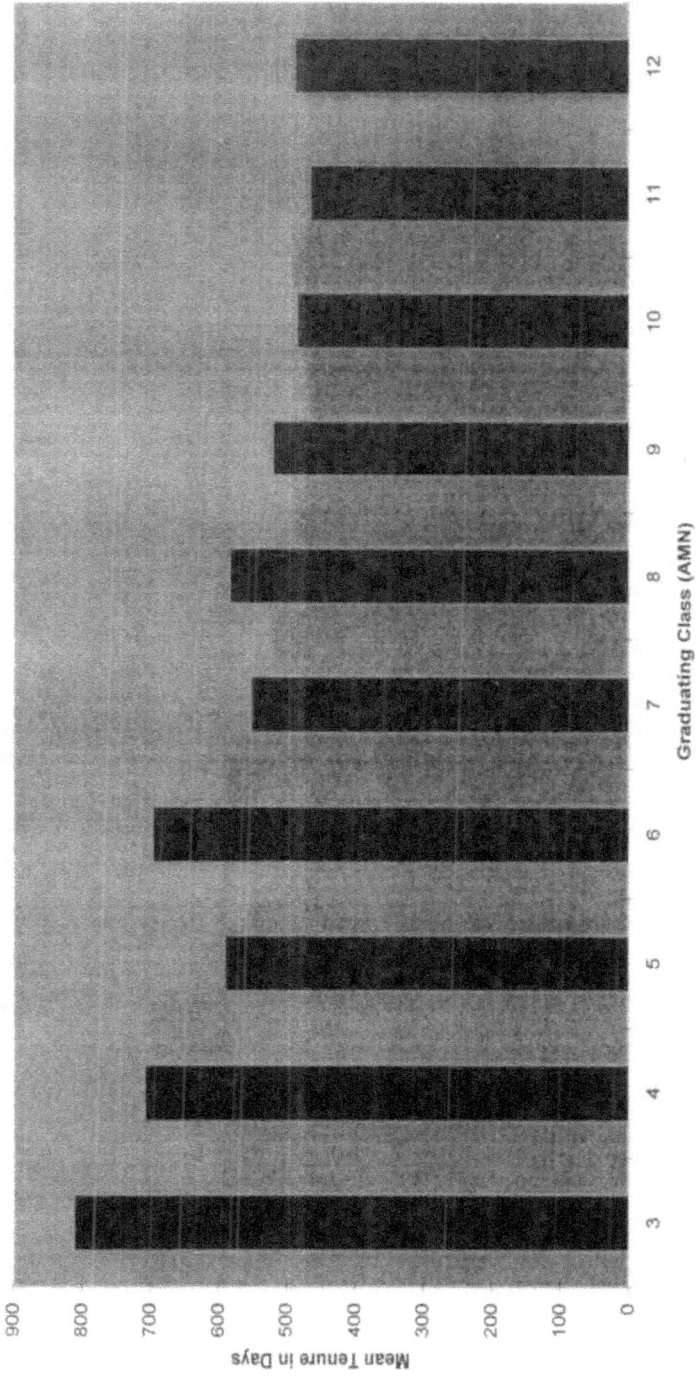

Figure 2.1: Mean Tenure for Korem Commanders by Graduating Class (AMN) (1984-1997)

Figure 2.2: Mean Tenure for Kodam Commanders by Graduating Class (AMN) (1965-1997)

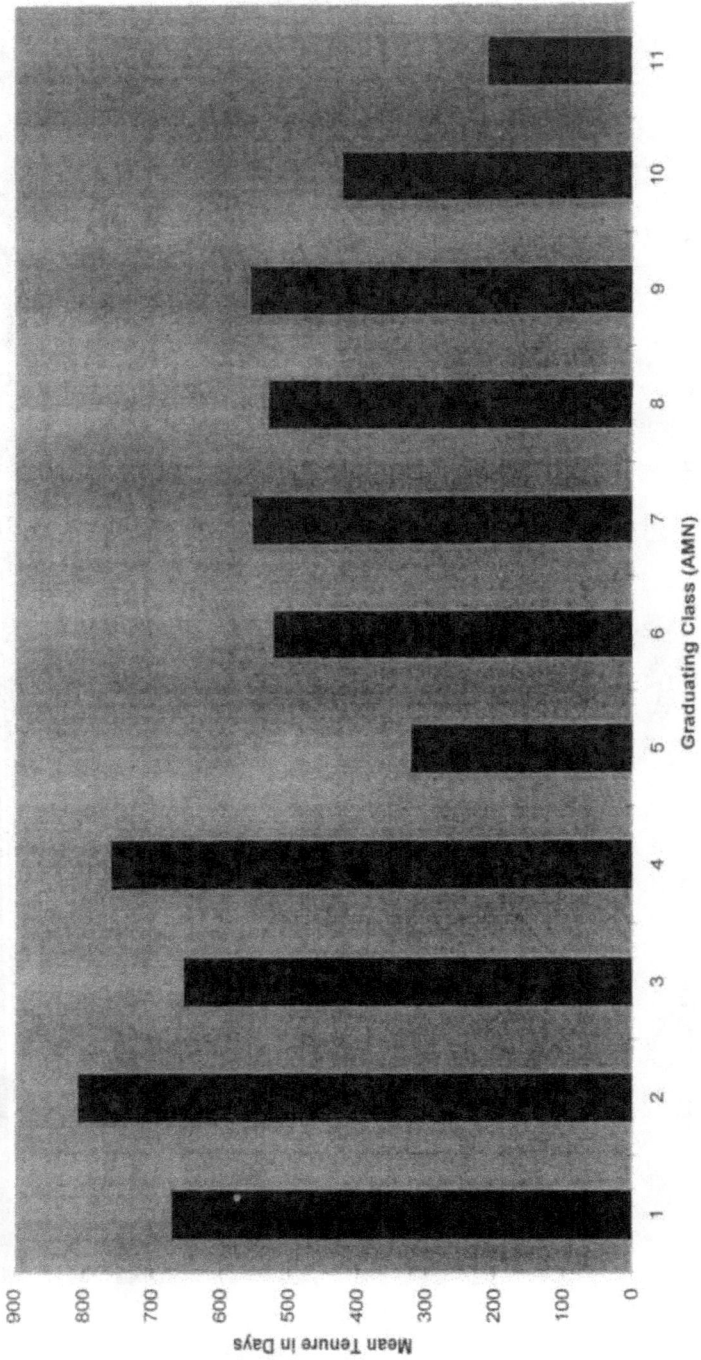

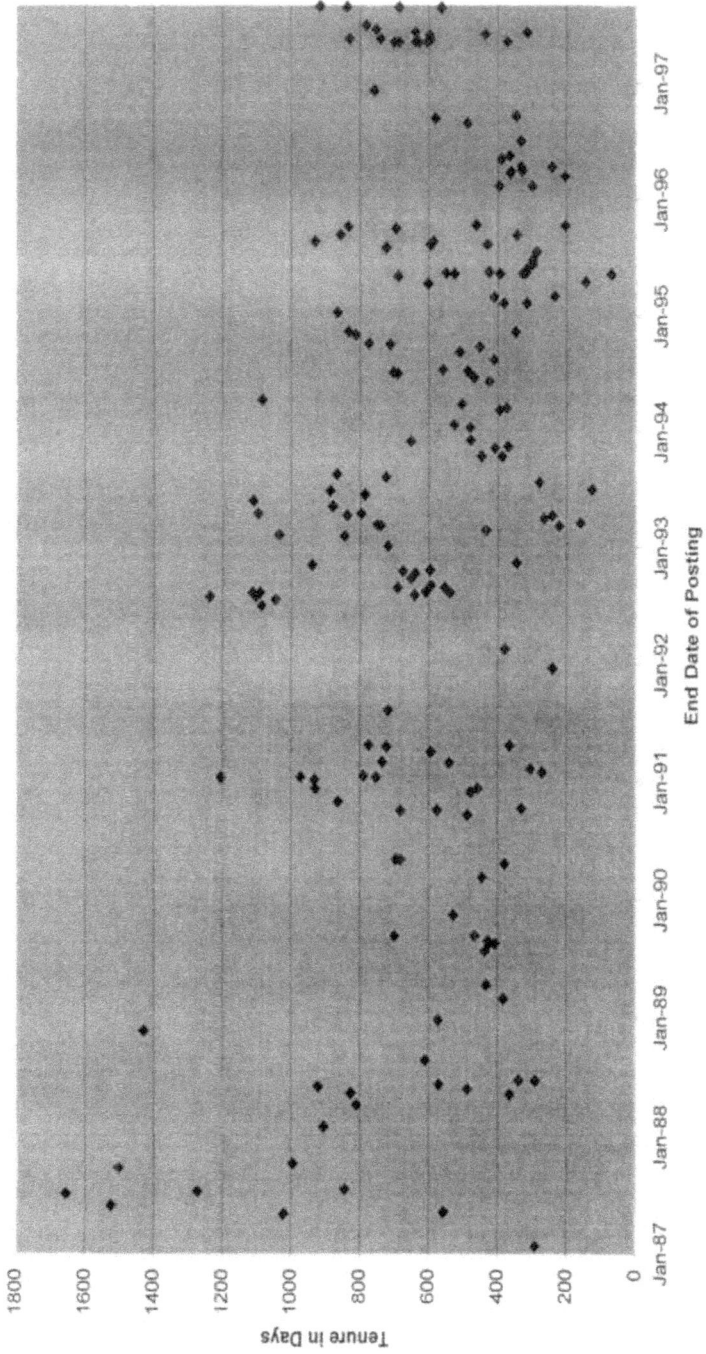

Figure 2.3: Tenure vs. End Date of Posting: Korem Commanders (1987–1997)

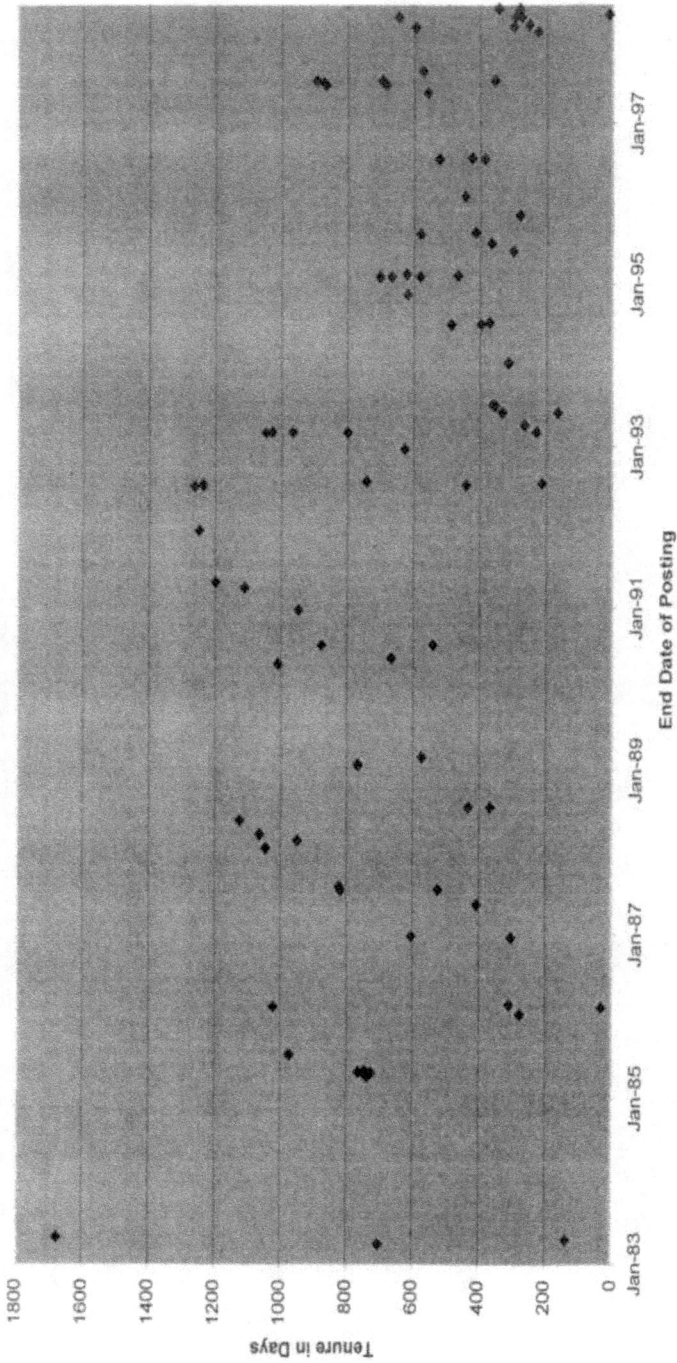

Figure 2.4: Tenure vs. End Date of Posting: Kodam Commanders (1983-1997)

MAPPING CAREER PATHS IN THE INDONESIAN ARMY

Having examined a number of structural features of the assignment and promotion process, it is now possible to turn to a broader consideration of career paths within the Indonesian Army. By what routes do officers rise in the Indonesian Army? What positions provide the best career opportunities? Path analysis of career trajectories within the Indonesian Army is of importance for two distinct but related reasons. First, it provides a basis for evaluating the careers of officers who do not make it to general rank.[21] This is precisely the category of Army personnel we have identified as suffering from the swollen size of the officer corps and whose career ambitions are unfulfilled. Second, analysis of "typical" career trajectories provides a basis against which to evaluate the career paths of officers who do make general rank (and who therefore belong to the military elite).

In a recent book, Ian MacFarling explains that one of his aims was to "create a generalized picture of a senior officer [in the Indonesian military] and to examine the various career paths that individuals could take to the top."[22] This aim, however, is never fulfilled. What MacFarling does, rather, is to provide a flow chart which summarizes the cross-functional links between Army officers. Unfortunately, many of the "links" in the chart are either wrong or misleading.[23] These problems stem from a misunderstanding of two principles. The first concerns the distinction between commissioned officers (Akabri graduates as well as Secapa graduates) and non-commissioned officers, and the

---

21 An analysis of career paths on the basis of biographies which are available for officers of general rank would, quite obviously, be flawed because the sample of selected officers would not be representative of the officer corps as a whole. This, however, is precisely the approach adopted by Ian MacFarling. See Ian MacFarling, *The Dual Function of the Indonesian Armed Forces: Military Politics in Indonesia* (Sydney: Australian Defence Studies Centre, The University of New South Wales, 1996), chapter eight.

22 Ibid., p. 9.

23 Ibid., p. 149. From bottom to top, we should note: (1) military academy graduates do not serve as Koramil (sub-district) commanders; (2) Koramil commanders are never assigned to a subsequent posting as company commanders in the "external" (read: Kostrad and Kopassus) defense stream; (3) it is unheard of for an officer to be transferred directly from a position as battalion commander to serve as a *Bupati* or *Walikota*; (4) *Bupati* and *Walikota* are never given a subsequent assignment as Korem commander (rather, the reverse is typically the case); (5) "ABRI company managing directors" are never appointed as governors; and so forth.

differing career opportunities available to each. The second concerns the relationship between the territorial structure of the Army and the civilian administrative (*kekaryaan*) positions to which military personnel are seconded. MacFarling wrongly assumes that Army officers can and do move back and forth between active duty and civilian service.[24]

The extensive data available on the Army officer corps makes possible a relatively detailed consideration of career paths. To accomplish this we might begin with a simple two-dimensional chart —the horizontal axis showing the territorial and combat units of the Army, and the vertical axis divided by rank from major to general.[25] Using this, it is possible to develop a career path analysis of officers who served in each of a number of key positions. For reasons that take into account political importance as well as elegance, this analysis will cover the ranks of major to general and will pay particular attention to the command positions (battalion, Kodim, Korem and Kodam) analyzed in chapter one.[26]

At the rank of major, we can show the positions to which officers are most commonly posted after having served as battalion commanders. The percentages in Figure 2.5 represent the frequency with which battalion commanders have been assigned to each of a number of common posts.[27] Over the past decade significant temporal variations appear. Between 1989 and 1993, during which time military academy graduates from Class 10 (1970) through Class 14 (1974) served as battalion commanders, only 50 percent of all battalion commanders enjoyed vertical movement (i.e. promotion in rank) in their subsequent posting. From 1994 until the present, however, during which time officers from the much smaller academy classes reached the rank of major, more than 65 percent of all officers enjoyed vertical movement in their subsequent posting. From

---

24 The only exception to this is that officers who have served in the Department of Defense (Hankam) may be reassigned to territorial or staff positions in the Army or Armed Forces headquarters. To our knowledge, only one officer (Zaenal Basri Palaguna) has ever returned from *kekaryaan* duty to become a Kodam commander. For a discussion of *kekaryaan* policy during the mid-1980s and practice over the past decade, see chapter three.

25 See Figure 2.8, this chapter.

26 The data are insufficient for detailed analysis below the rank of major. Note that officers commonly make major during their mid-thirties.

27 These and all subsequent figures are for officers who were given a subsequent posting in active duty; it therefore excludes officers who are given *kekaryaan* service (for which the data are very sparse).

this we can conclude that short-term career prospects improved for majors during the mid-1990s and that the primary beneficiaries of this were members of the small post-1975 classes from the military academy.

At the level of Kodim commander (the holders of which are "senior" majors or "junior" lieutenant colonels), path analysis (see Figure 2.6) reveals that horizontal movement is the rule and vertical movement (i.e. promotion in rank) is virtually unknown. This breakdown provides a useful guide to the subsequent career success of officers. Most officers who have enjoyed rapid career promotion have done so via posting as Deputy Assistant (*wakil asisten*) at Kodam headquarters. By contrast, reassignment as a Kodim commander or subsequent assignment to either *pabandya* staff positions at Kodam headquarters[28] or to a Chief of Staff position for a Korem commander (Kasrem) signals career stagnation. These assignments are most commonly followed by early retirement and posting in a *kekaryaan* function at the district or provincial level. A similar divide holds for rural- versus urban-based Kodim commanders: officers serving in urban centers or their peripheral territorial units have enjoyed far greater promotional success than have officers posted in rural areas.

---

28 This covers *Perwira Bantuan Madya* (Pabandya), i.e. lower middle-ranking officers seconded to Chiefs of Staff.

Figure 2.5: Subsequent Assignment of Battalion Commanders, 1989-1997

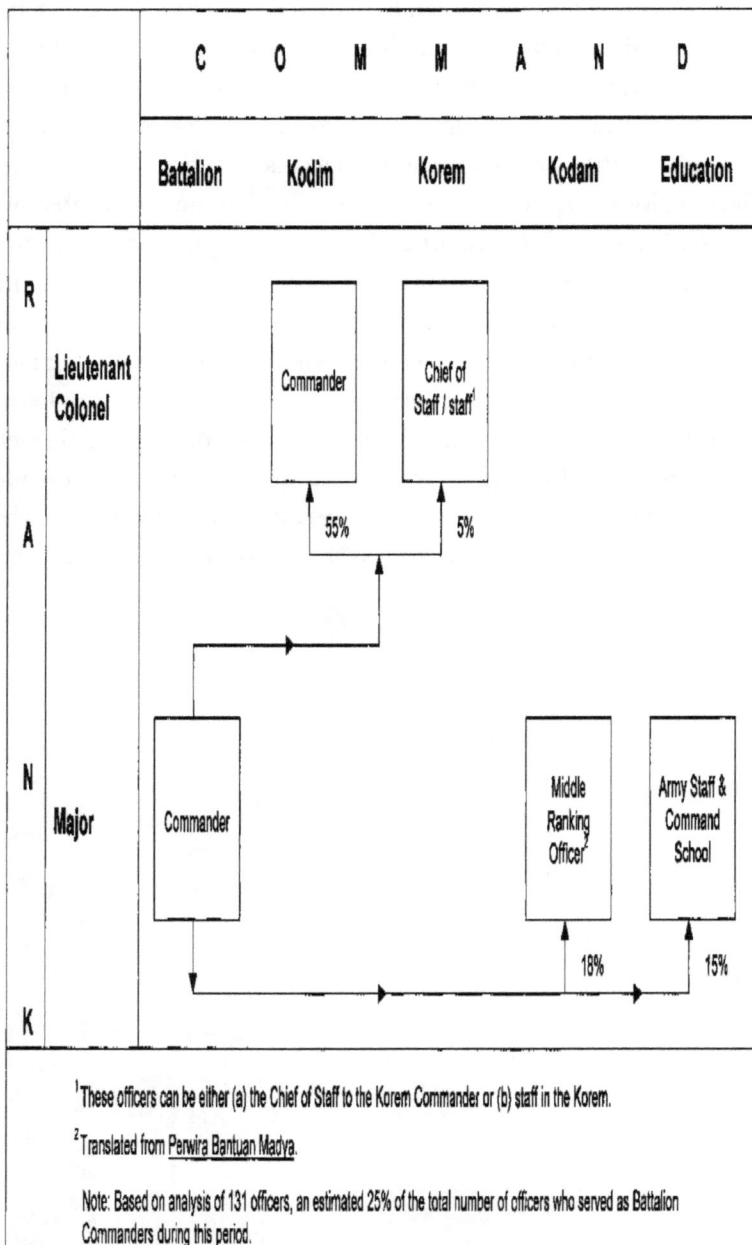

[1] These officers can be either (a) the Chief of Staff to the Korem Commander or (b) staff in the Korem.

[2] Translated from Perwira Bantuan Madya.

Note: Based on analysis of 131 officers, an estimated 25% of the total number of officers who served as Battalion Commanders during this period.

Figure 2.6: Subsequent Assignment of Kodim Commanders, 1989-1997

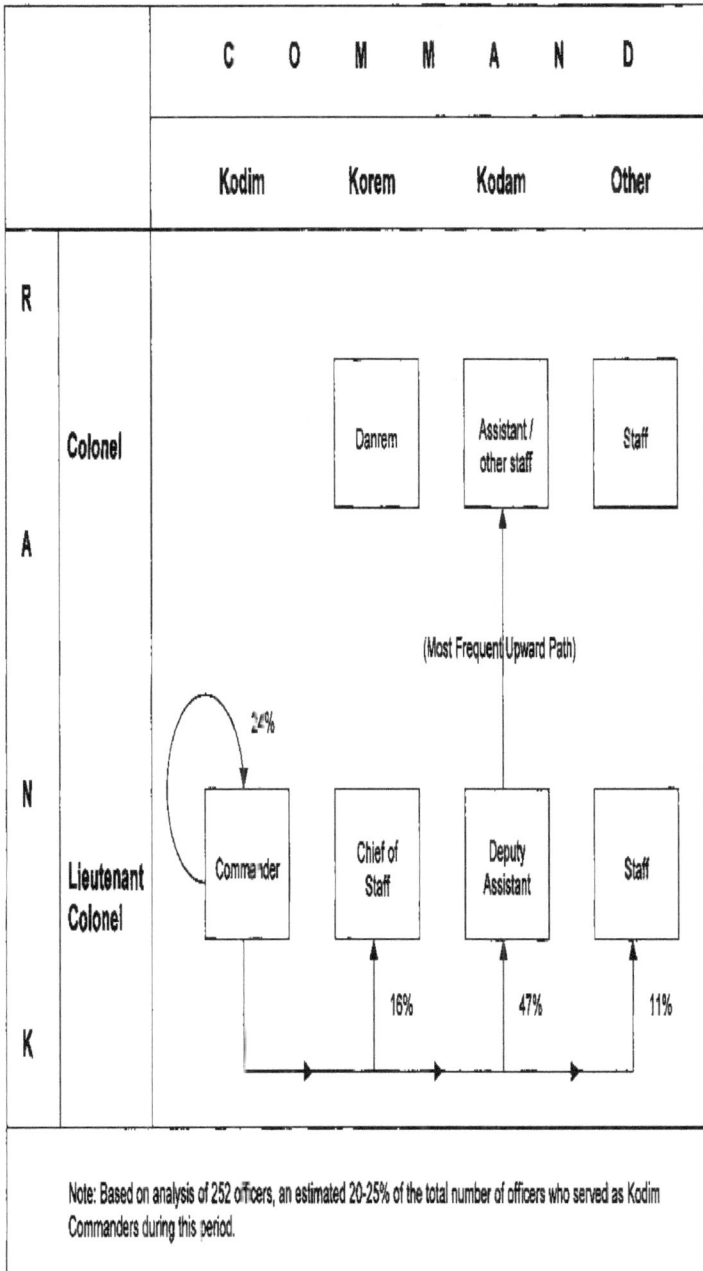

Note: Based on analysis of 252 officers, an estimated 20-25% of the total number of officers who served as Kodim Commanders during this period.

The most difficult and most important promotion in rank in the Indonesian Army is from colonel to brigadier general. Of the roughly four hundred to five hundred active colonels in the Indonesian Army, an estimated one in four is promoted to brigadier general (while on active duty).[29] As discussed in chapter one, at the time of the 1985 reorganization of the Army, ABRI Commander-in-Chief Benny Moerdani mentioned that the thirty-nine new-style Korem would be the testing grounds for the future Army elite. It is worth re-evaluating this prediction in light of our current analysis of career paths. A close look at officers who completed a tour of duty as Korem commander between 1990 and 1997 (198 individuals) reveals that *at least* 41 percent were subsequently promoted to brigadier general. Given the large number of officers for whom such identifications cannot be made, this figure can safely be increased to 50 percent. An assignment as a Korem commander thus doubles an officer's odds of making it to general rank. This clearly suggests that Moerdani's intention of having the new-style Korem serve as a testing ground for promotion to general rank has indeed been implemented.

What, then, are the most common career moves (for officers who remain on active duty) after serving as a Korem commander? The path analysis in Figure 2.7 reveals four typical assignments: as Chief of Staff to a Kodam commander, as a command or staff officer with the Army Strategic Command, or as a staff officer at either Armed Forces or Army headquarters in the capital. As is so often the case, the less common command assignments are normally preferable to the staff postings.

The significance of these routes is best highlighted by considering the next command level within the Army—the level occupied by the ten powerful Kodam commanders. Analysis of the positions held by officers immediately prior to assignment as Kodam commanders reveals the following breakdown: 40 percent had previously served as Kodam Chief of Staff, 21 percent had previously served in Army headquarters, 12 percent had previously served in Kostrad, and the remainder had come from Armed Forces headquarters, Special Forces, and the Department of Defense (Departemen Pertahanan dan Keamanan).

---

29 Officers on *kekaryaan* duty also remain eligible for, and commonly receive, promotion. These officers, however, are never reassigned to active military duty.

Finally, we can consider briefly the subsequent posting of officers who served as Kodam commanders. Over the past eight years, one-third of all Kodam commanders were reassigned to posts in ABRI headquarters, most as assistants to the Chief of Staff, with the rank of major general or lieutenant general. Other Kodam commanders were subsequently posted at Army headquarters (15 percent), given *kekaryaan* duty as members of national parliament or provincial governor (24 percent), or retired from service altogether (31 percent).

Combining these tiered analyses, we can now provide an overview of career moves within the Army. In Figure 2.8, we have highlighted the most common transfers and promotions for each of the four strategic commands. While each of these steps represents the most likely career path of an upwardly mobile officer, the likelihood that any one officer has followed *all* of the steps in this path is extremely low. The importance of this analysis is that it provides a rough but useful estimate of the odds that an officer in a given position will enjoy horizontal versus vertical promotion. Furthermore, it suggests that at any given point in their careers, Army officers should have a reasonably good understanding of their own career prospects. As will be discussed in the next chapter, this plays a central role in explaining the expectations, behavior, and political outlook within the officer corps.

Figure 2.7: Subsequent Assignment of Korem Commanders, 1989-1997

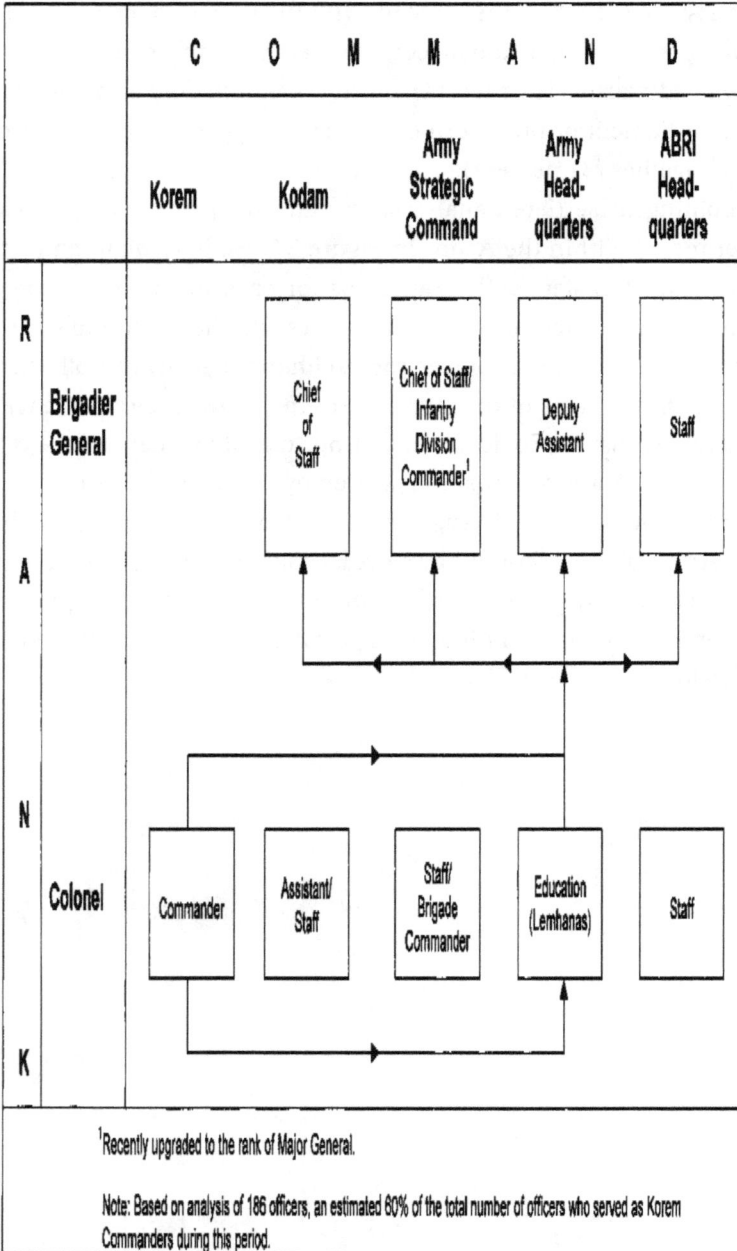

		C O M M A N D			
		Korem	Kodam	Army Strategic Command	Army Head-quarters	ABRI Head-quarters

Brigadier General — Chief of Staff (Kodam); Chief of Staff/Infantry Division Commander[1] (Army Strategic Command); Deputy Assistant (Army Headquarters); Staff (ABRI Headquarters)

Colonel — Commander (Korem); Assistant/Staff (Kodam); Staff/Brigade Commander (Army Strategic Command); Education (Lemhanas) (Army Headquarters); Staff (ABRI Headquarters)

[1]Recently upgraded to the rank of Major General.

Note: Based on analysis of 186 officers, an estimated 80% of the total number of officers who served as Korem Commanders during this period.

Figure 2.8: Assignment and Promotion Patterns within the Indonesian Army[1]

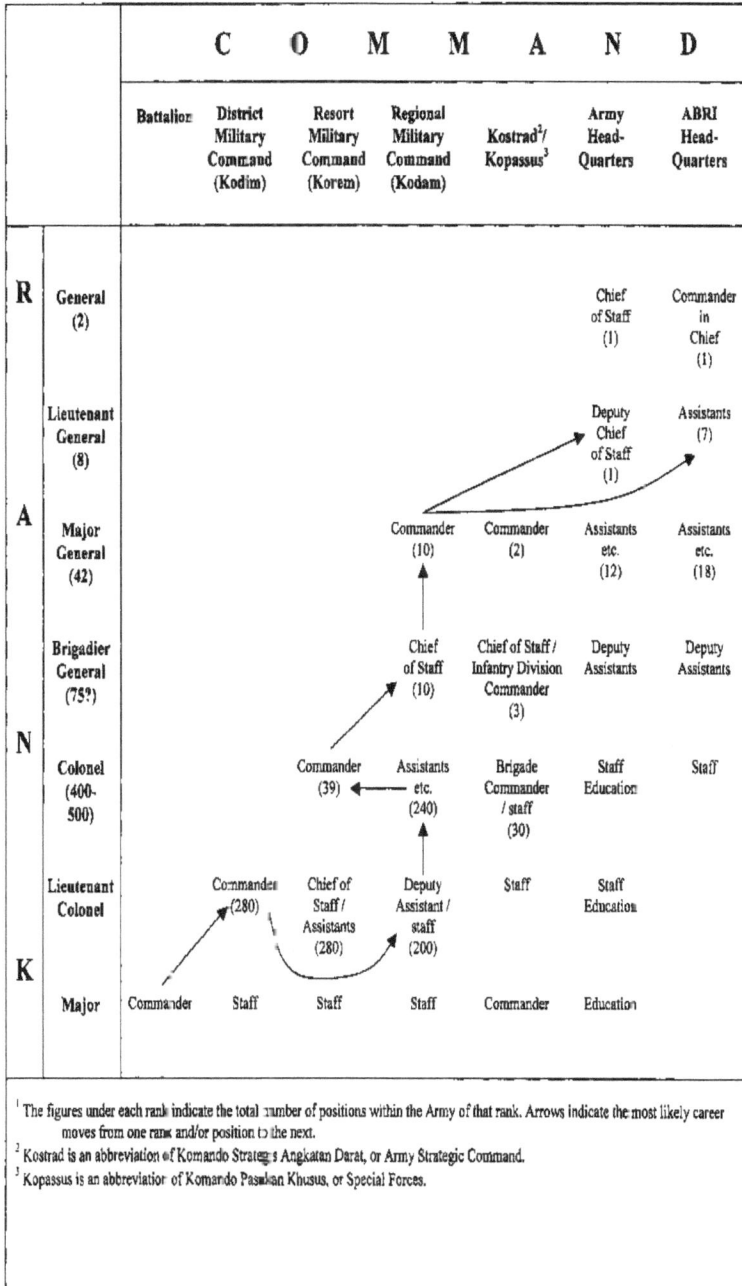

	Battalion	District Military Command (Kodim)	Resort Military Command (Korem)	Regional Military Command (Kodam)	Kostrad[2]/ Kopassus[3]	Army Head-Quarters	ABRI Head-Quarters
R **General** (2)						Chief of Staff (1)	Commander in Chief (1)
Lieutenant General (8)					Deputy Chief of Staff (1)		Assistants (7)
A **Major General** (42)				Commander (10)	Commander (2)	Assistants etc. (12)	Assistants etc. (18)
Brigadier General (75?)				Chief of Staff (10)	Chief of Staff / Infantry Division Commander (3)	Deputy Assistants	Deputy Assistants
N **Colonel** (400-500)			Commander (39)	Assistants etc. (240)	Brigade Commander /staff (30)	Staff Education	Staff
Lieutenant Colonel		Commander (280)	Chief of Staff / Assistants (280)	Deputy Assistant / staff (200)	Staff	Staff Education	
K **Major**	Commander	Staff	Staff	Staff	Commander	Education	

[1] The figures under each rank indicate the total number of positions within the Army of that rank. Arrows indicate the most likely career moves from one rank and/or position to the next.

[2] Kostrad is an abbreviation of Komando Strategis Angkatan Darat, or Army Strategic Command.

[3] Kopassus is an abbreviation of Komando Pasukan Khusus, or Special Forces.

CONCLUSION

In this chapter we have argued that common perceptions of the promotional process in the Indonesian Army are at best inadequate. This is not to deny that there are individual officers who have enjoyed exceptional career success because of familial ties or their personal connections to senior government and military figures. But when one studies an institution as large as the Indonesian Army, it would be a mistake to generalize from a few, highly visible examples to draw conclusions about the entire officer corps. We have demonstrated the importance of structural features of the officer corps in the process of assignment and promotion in the Army, and in particular the impact of recommendations by classmates and the effect of class solidarity.

This analysis allows us to refine the basic model explaining changing command tenure presented in chapter one. Whereas chapter one argued that decreasing command tenure within the Indonesian Army was necessitated by the changing size of the officer corps, we can now supplement our analysis by taking into account the monopolization of command positions by particular cohorts from the military academy. The sharp drop in command tenure in particular and the tour of duty for Army officers in general was, thus, a response to two related factors: the increase in the size of the officer corps and the extraordinary success of one class from the military academy.

During the 1990s, however, the Indonesian Army responded to these structural dilemmas by adopting a number of corrective measures and standardizing the appointment process. Each cohort from the military academy is now being allocated roughly equal numbers of command positions. The overall tenure for these different cohorts has more or less been equalized. These policy corrections are underscored by the narrowing of variability in command tenure at several levels over the past decade. These moves have, in turn, created relatively stable career paths which, for better or for worse, became increasingly visible to members of the officer corps.

IMPLICATIONS OF STRUCTURAL CHANGE FOR MILITARY POLITICS

When Indonesian Army officers are asked about their prospects for future assignments or their willingness to be assigned to a particular post, they invariably offer the same rehearsed response: it is not a question of what an officer would like or dislike, they repeat, but of what their commanders require. In response to speculation about his reassignment as a Kodam commander, a Major General in the elite Army Strategic Command (Kostrad) recently offered this exaggerated but not atypical comment:

> A soldier doesn't need to be asked if he is prepared to be posted somewhere or not, but rather what the orders are from the Commander-in-Chief and the Army Chief of Staff. As soldiers, we are always ready; if there was a position for us in hell and we were assigned there, then we'd be prepared.[1]

This is telling testimony to the ethos of professionalism and duty instilled at the military academy and maintained within the active officer corps. But whether they foresee themselves ordered to a post as commander in hell or to a cushy staff position in Army headquarters, Army officers are all too aware that assignments and career prospects are not simply a matter of institutional requirements.

The accordion-like expansion and contraction in the number of cadets

---

1 Brigadier General Djamari Chaniago, quoted in "Situasi politik secara nasional sudah mereda, " *Angkatan Bersenjata*, July 11, 1997.

graduated from the National Military Academy and the corresponding variation in the size of the Army's commissioned officer corps have obvious and immediate implications for officers' career prospects. This, of course, is of fundamental importance to military politics in the 1990s. These changes have both presented the Army leadership with significant new opportunities as well as posed a series of serious dilemmas. This chapter traces the ways in which ABRI has responded to the swollen size of some echelons of the commissioned officer corps and explores some of the implications that these responses have had on the political role of the Army. Because of the limited material available about the internal dynamics of the Army and difficulties in documenting deviations from military norms, the analysis developed here is necessarily of a provisional nature. We hope, however, that an exploration of the logical implications of these structural changes will complement existing sources and analyses.

SPECIALISTS

> In order to economize on finances and effort, [military] education will direct personnel into particular fields.
> - ABRI Commander-in-Chief B. L. Moerdani, 1985[2]

Like all militaries, the Indonesian Army has a number of service branches —infantry, cavalry, engineering, adjutant general, and so forth —based on both combat and staff specializations. The burgeoning size of the officers corps reaching middle ranks during the late 1980s and early 1990s made possible new kinds of specialization in response to challenges emanating from civil society.

In this regard, the extensive Army intelligence apparatus is of special interest. At the Kodam level, the Assistant for Intelligence (*Asintel Kasdam*) has under his command an Intelligence Detachment Commander (*Danden Intel*, with the rank of lieutenant colonel), who in turn oversees the operations of four intelligence specialists (with the rank of major or lieutenant colonel). These officers are responsible for issues concerning mass mobilization, research, logistics, and personnel

---

2 "ABRI Tahun 2000, Seperti Apa?" *Tempo*, May 4, 1985.

placement and welfare.[3] In contrast to the overall tendency within the Armed Forces, where service in intelligence generally helps pave the route to career advancement, the limited information available suggests that these "specialists" have not enjoyed promotional or career mobility. After serving as intelligence specialists, most of these officers have been appointed to serve as Kodim commanders in strategic or problematic areas, but have not then risen to higher or more prestigious posts.[4] The military's need for staff with specialized training, knowledge, and experience may relegate these officers to operationally important posts while paradoxically hindering vertical career movement.

Functional specialization within the officer corps is most apparent and most easily documented in relation to the rising tide of industrial conflict during the 1990s. During this time, it has become increasingly common for officers who serve in industrial regions, and who consequently have experience intervening in industrial conflicts and "safeguarding" against labor protest, to be transferred to other industrial regions. In 1992, for example, the section head for intelligence in Tangerang (*Kepala Seksi Intel* Kodim 0506), Major Barusanusi, was transferred to serve as section head for intelligence in Surabaya (Korem 084). As one of the earliest and most important centers of industrial unrest, Kodim 0506 Tangerang was one of the first to develop expertise in handling strikes. With the re-emergence of industrial strikes in the greater Surabaya region beginning in 1991, Major Barusanusi brought with him the system of industrial surveillance first developed in Tangerang.[5] The career paths of officers such as Major Barusanusi provide strong evidence that the Army has responded to industrial strikes through the development of and reliance on "specialists" trained to handle industrial relations. For many of these

---

3   The abbreviated titles are: *Pabandya Gal Sinteldam, Pabandya Lit, Pabandya Mat Slogdam,* and *Pabandya Lurja Jahril.* It would be interesting to know when and why these positions were first created. The best work on the Indonesian military intelligence apparatus does not mention these positions. This may be because these positions are recent additions to the Kodam structure. See Richard Tanter, "Intelligence Agencies and Third World Militarization: A Case Study of Indonesia, 1966-1989" (PhD dissertation, Monash University, 1991).

4   These observations are based primarily on data for Kodam V Brawijaya (East Java), for which the most extensive personnel data are available. Curiously, in September 1997 the new commander of Kodam V, Major General Djadja Suparman, commented that the number of intelligence officers at the Kodam level was insufficient. See "Pangdam: Jumlah Intel Kodam Masih Kurang, " *Surabaya Post,* September 9, 1997.

5   We are grateful to Munir for this information.

officers, however, specialization has meant the sidetracking of career ambitions and promotion.

For other officers, the experiences and new skills developed while serving in industrial areas have been stepping stones for further career advancement. In this regard, we can cite a host of officers who served as Battalion or Kodim commanders in densely industrial regions and who have since enjoyed rapid career advancement and assignment to strategic and highly desirable posts.[6] Several examples can be listed briefly:

> *Sumardi*: Served as Commander of the 203rd Infantry Battalion in Tangerang (? - 1989), Commander of Kodim 0507 Bekasi (1989-91), Deputy Assistant of Operations in Kodam Jaya (1991-92), and then as Commander of the Kodam Jaya Infantry Brigade (1992-93); he was subsequently transferred to command the industrially-strategic Korem 084 Surabaya (1994-95); served as Commander of the Kostrad 2nd Infantry Brigade in Malang, East Java (1995); rose to Chief of Staff of Kodam III Siliwangi (1995-97), in heavily industrial West Java. In July 1997 he was promoted to serve as Commander of the Infantry Weapons Center in Bandung (Dan Pussenif).
>
> *R. R. Simbolon*: Served as the Commander of the 203rd Infantry Battalion in Tangerang (1991) and as Commander of the Tangerang 0506 Military District Command (1991-93). He was then appointed Deputy Assistant for Operations in Kodam Jaya (1993-94), and subsequently became Commander of the Kodam Jaya Infantry Brigade (1994-96). It was from this position that his predecessor, Sumardi, was promoted to the Surabaya 084 Korem, and a similar appointment to command in an industrial center would not be surprising.

At least seven other officers with similar career backgrounds serving in industrial regions have risen to become Korem commanders. Slamet Supriadi served as Kodim commander and in intelligence positions in

---

6   A tour of duty in an industrial area holds its own appeal: involvement in overseeing industrial relations and settling labor disputes is normally accompanied by significant financial remuneration. Financial resources, in turn, may be used to "influence" or even "buy" a desirable reassignment.

Jakarta before being promoted to command Korem 074 Surakarta in 1994, just as Surakarta was first affected by strikes. Djoko Mulono served as commander of the Bekasi and Bogor Kodim before rising to command Korem 063 Cirebon, another industrially sensitive region. Sutarto SK was promoted from Security Assistant of the Jakarta Garrison to the post of Assistant for Intelligence in Kodam V Brawijaya (East Java), and then to commander of Korem 084 Surabaya. Similarly, Syamsul Ma'arif rose from local battalion and Kodim commander in Surabaya to become commander of Korem 084 Surabaya. Finally, Colonels Sunarto and Syarnubi both were transferred from industrially sensitive positions to command Korem 022, Pematang Siantar, following the April 1994 labor demonstrations and riots in Medan, North Sumatra.

These observations suggest a shift in the career trajectories of Army officers rising to the top regional command positions. Observers of the Indonesian military have long noted that (successful) service in the East Timor campaign was a crucial testing ground for the promotion of military officers.[7] This, however, may no longer be as important as it once was, both due to the shift from armed resistance to urban protest in East Timor and because of the emergence of new social movements in Indonesian society. Rather, during the 1990s service in industrial regions and the consequent development of special experience in "handling" or "quelling" civilian unrest has become an increasingly important avenue for career advancement.

This political specialization within the commissioned officer corps was made possible, at least in part, by the increased number of officers reaching middle ranks during the late 1980s and early 1990s. But while specialization within the officer corps provided the Army with a means of responding to new and increasingly radical forms of protest and civil unrest, it has had a mixed effect on the officer corps itself. For some officers, service in industrial centers has proven to be a significant qualification for further promotion, while for many middle-ranking officers "tracking" as a trouble-shooter or area specialist has meant career stagnation.

---

7   See, for example, The Editors, "Current Data on the Indonesian Military Elite: January 1, 1992 - August 31, 1993, " *Indonesia* 56 (October 1993): 126.

OFFICERS IN THE DARK?

A Kodim commander must be able to lead troops and also to master territorial problems...He must be able to handle flare-ups without shooting. He must be able to handle disputes without giving rise to flare-ups.

- ABRI Commander-in-Chief B. L. Moerdani, 1985[8]

The decrease in mean command tenure also has important implications for internal military dynamics and local politics. For as command tenure changes, so too do the abilities and expectations of the officer corps. To understand this, one must bear in mind that commanders typically serve far shorter terms than do the staff officers who serve under them. Territorial commanders therefore frequently depend on the knowledge and require the cooperation of their local staff. The seven primary assistants[9] and other personnel in the Kodim and Korem offices include fellow commissioned officers from the military academy, Secapa graduates, and a host of non-commissioned personnel of lower ranks. The acceleration of transfers and reduction of command tenure has important implications for these command-staff relations. As command tenure decreases, it is likely that the staff in Kodim and Korem units will come to perceive newly appointed commanders as being privileged by virtue of education alone (and that, often enough, a result of family background). Serving a brief tour of duty, these officers do not necessarily have the opportunity to demonstrate professional military know-how to an other than skeptical command staff. Similarly, during a short tour of duty as Kodim or Korem commander, these officers may not accord sufficient attention to the material welfare of their subordinates.

For permanent staff, this game of musical chairs is a mixed-bag. On the one hand, the rapid replacement of commanders further ensures their dependence on knowledgeable local staff. On the other hand, it is not hard to imagine situations in which frustrated staff with little or no hope of advancement might withhold information or complicate the duties of

---

8   "ABRI Tahun 2000, Seperti Apa?" *Tempo*, May 4, 1985.
9   These assistants cover intelligence, operations, personnel, logistics, planning, territorial affairs, and social and political affairs.

a commanding officer who is seen to be on the fast track. The emergence of friction between commanding officers and their staff or troops is all the more likely given the extremely low salaries and official remuneration within the military and the exceptional levels of corruption, bribery, and racketeering within the military. Where a commissioned officer with bright career prospects might wish to protect his reputation and run a clean unit, locally based personnel with few or no promotional prospects may be intent on enriching themselves and asserting their social power.[10] Stern disciplinary measures taken by either local territorial commanders or Army leadership to prevent such abuses are only likely to exacerbate these tensions.

In addition to establishing good working relations with their staff and securing the respect of troops whom they command, newly appointed territorial commanders must also develop a wide network of community contacts. This commonly involves meetings with the leaders of the political parties and mass organizations, visits to influential religious teachers (*kyai, ulama,* priests and pastors), as well as speeches to university students, artists, non-governmental organizations, and the like. So important is this practice that a number of territorial commanders have made the "coffee morning" a daily routine, inviting prominent figures (*tokoh masyarakat*) to their headquarters and even to their homes for discussions and not-so-subtle cooptation. On these visits, territorial Army commanders seek to open channels of communication and foster acceptance of the Army's role in civilian affairs.

But it takes time for an Army officer to visit all of the relevant organizations and attend local social functions. The less time an officer has served in a given position, the less time he will have had to establish these networks of information and control and, by extension, the less able he will be to prevent the occurrence of disturbances and unrest. Because of the obvious difficulties in determining when local Kodim and battalion commanders were appointed, it is not possible to comment

---

10 Although we do not have a single study of racketeering within the military, this has been cited as an important element of military politics in East Timor. See The Editors, "Current Data on the Indonesian Military Elite: July 1, 1989-January 1, 1992, " *Indonesia* 53 (April 1992): 98-99. The problem is best attested to by the frequency with which members of the Army elite issue warnings about the severe punishment awaiting ABRI personnel found guilty of *beking* (backing) gambling, entertainment, and other illegal businesses.

with any certainty on how many of the riots of the past two years have in fact occurred in locations with newly appointed commanders.[11] Suffice it to say, the rise in open political violence and riots of the past three years has come at precisely the time when command tenures of local military commanders have plummeted to their lowest levels. When local disturbances do occur, local military commanders who have only served for a short time, and therefore not yet established a wide network of contacts and relationships, will have a more difficult time in eliciting the cooperation of local figures in quelling unrest and assuring the local population that the case will be handled fairly. This dynamic has been highlighted during a number of the riots over the past year; following these disturbances, the press has reported (often with apparent delight) that Kodim and Korem commanders have needed to request the intervention of local religious figures to help restore order.[12]

Just as the reduction of average tenure for territorial commanders may increase the likelihood that social unrest will take the form of public violence, the occurrence of riots and political violence has had a reciprocal effect on command tenure. When riots do occur, local military commanders are frequently relieved of their assignment. There are a number of reasons for this. First, Army leaders may hold a local commander accountable for the disturbance or choose to set an example of stern discipline. Second, an officer may be transferred for his own protection. And third, an officer may be transferred so as to reduce local anger at military personnel who (rightly or wrongly) are perceived to be responsible for the incident in question. Soon after the October 1996 riots in Situbondo, for example, the local Kodim commander, Lieutenant Colonel Imam Prawoto, was transferred after having served for a mere eight months. Official statements that Prawoto's transfer was not related to the riots only confirmed the need to assuage local anger at the military's handling of the situation.[13] While it is impossible to gauge how

---

11 For a study of the relationship between violence and leadership tenure at the national level, see Guy D. Whitten and Henry S. Bienen, "Political Violence and Time in Power, " *Armed Forces and Society* 23, 2 (Winter 1996): 209-234.

12 Unrest, of course, is not limited to areas where the military command is newly appointed. Shortly, we will also argue that particularly long tours of duty for local military commanders may also play a contributing factor in local disturbances.

13 Indeed, one newspaper reported that, according to the Kodam commander, Prawoto was

frequently officers are transferred prematurely because of local unrest, unprofessional conduct, or the military's desire to designate a scapegoat, there can be little doubt that such moves have contributed to the recent reduction of Kodim (and perhaps also battalion) command tenure.

SHIFTING CAREER PROSPECTS

It will indeed be more difficult to become a colonel, a brigadier general, a major general. That's true. The reason is that where there were once ten officers fighting for five posts, in the future there might be 100 officers fighting [for the same five posts].
- ABRI Commander-in-Chief B. L. Moerdani, 1985[14]

Variations in the size of the officer corps and the resulting reduction in command tenure also have a direct and immediate impact on promotional and career prospects for Army officers. For the Army, when any given class at the military academy includes a relatively large number of cadets, there will necessarily be more intense competition for desirable assignments and promotions among those cadets. Competition within the officer corps is thus seen as a healthy means of encouraging professionalism and evaluating officers' performance. Indeed, in an interview following the 1985 Army reorganization, ABRI Commander-in-Chief Benny Moerdani noted with satisfaction that in the future there would be intense competition between hundreds of colonels for a limited number of positions at general rank.[15] For military academy graduates, however, small class size makes for better career prospects while large cohort size makes for poorer promotional prospects as more officers compete for the same small number of desired posts.

To evaluate the impact of class size on career advancement, ideally one would like to be able to compare the collective success of each graduating class from the military academy. To do so, however, would require

experiencing "stress. " and that this was problematic in light of the upcoming election. See "Pangdam V Brawijaya: Suhu Politik Mulai Memanas, " *Jawa Pos*, December 14, 1996.

14 "Reorganisasi, tapi bukan rasioralisasi, " *Tempo*, May 4, 1985.

15 Interview with General Moerdani, "ABRI Tahun 2000, Seperti Apa?" *Tempo*, May 4, 1985, pp. 16-17.

identifying the position(s) held by each officer and then creating a system by which to "score" the rank or positions these officers hold, an exercise impossible without access to complete Army records. Alternatively, one could compare the number of officers from each class who achieve a given rank (major, lieutenant colonel, etc.). A far easier, and perhaps more revealing, method is to calculate the number of officers from each AMN class who were appointed to key territorial command positions at different levels.

Comparison of the number of officers from each AMN class who served as Kodam commander (Pangdam) reveals a wide disparity in class success (see Table 3.1). The members of AMN Classes 1 (1960) through 3 (1962) enjoyed the benefits of prestige attached to the new academy and their relatively small cohort size, earning from five to nine appointments per class. Classes 4 (1963) and 5 (1964), by contrast, enjoyed far less success at this level, with fewer and a smaller percentage of officers in each class becoming Pangdam. Following a long period during which the extremely large and exceptionally successful Class 6 (1965) exerted a strangle-hold on advancement, the classes of the late 1960s fared far less well. Classes 10 (1970) and 11 (1971) were the greatest beneficiaries of the sweeping post-1997 election personnel changes, but will most likely not receive further appointments. The remaining large classes of the early 1970s will certainly receive further Kodam commands, though it seems unlikely that they will fare any better than class 10 (1970) or Class 11 (1971) and may, in fact, fare significantly worse. Overall, therefore, we can see that an officer's chance of becoming Pangdam has dropped from 8 percent to 2 percent over the past fifteen years.

Analysis of the number of officers from each class to serve as Korem commander (Danrem) is equally revealing. The available data are poor for Classes 1 and 2, the members of which served as Danrem during the late 1970s and early 1980s, and must therefore be excluded from our analysis. At the other end of the spectrum, Classes 10 through 13 will most likely not be given additional Danremships, and so can be included, while subsequent classes will receive additional appointments and thus must be held out of the current analysis. This provides us with a span of eleven classes on which to base our observations. Although there is a tremendous bulge in the number of officers from Class 6 (1965) appointed to serve as Korem commander (fifty-six), the class percentage is in fact no

higher than that for Classes 3 (1962) and 4 (1963), and lower than that for
the much smaller Class 8 (1967). Subsequent classes, however, have seen
a significant drop in both the total number of officers and the percentage
of the cohort appointed to serve as Korem commander. Again, over a
ten year span, the odds of an officer being appointed Korem commander
have dropped by 75 percent.

Table 3.1:
Korem and Kodam Commanders by AMN Class

Year	Class	Class Size	Danrem Total	Danrem Percent	Pangdam** Total	Pangdam** Percent
1960	1	59	na	na	5	8.4%
1961	2	151	na	na	9	5.9%
1962	3	112	15	13.4%	9	8.0%
1963	4	113	15	13.4%	4	3.5%
1964	5	280	10	3.5%	3	1.0%
1965	6	433	56	12.9%	14	3.2%
1966	7	243	21	8.6%	6	2.4%
1967	8	203	29	14.2%	3	1.8%
1968	9	465	20	4.2%	3	0.6%
1969	no class					
1970	10	437	20	4.6%	8	1.8%
1971	11	329	27	8.2%	8	2.4%
1972	12	389	23	5.9%	2*	-
1973	13	436	19	4.3%	1ˠ	-
1974	14	434	15*	-	2ˠ	-
1975	15	304	6*	-	-	-

n.a. = not available

* Will receive additional appointments

** A decade ago it was not uncommon for a Major General to serve as
Pangdam in more than one location, something that is now unheard of.
We have taken this into account in the above calculations, which thus
reflect the total number of officers, not the number of posts held.[16]

---

16 Note: because of the difficulty of identifying the holders of these positions, the same analysis is not

The deterioration of career prospects resulting from the burgeoning size of the officer corps has important implications for officers' performance and for local security. As their prospects for future appointments and promotions deteriorate, Army officers may become reluctant to take an activist role or a hard-line position on local issues. This is particularly true among middle-ranking officers (e.g. the lieutenant colonels and colonels who command and staff Kodim and Korem units). Although successful intervention in a pressing or potentially explosive local dispute may still lead to career advancement, there is in fact no guarantee that an officer will be rewarded for such actions. Lieutenant Colonel Djasmin Senos is an excellent example. During the longer than average period (thirty-two months) in which he served as commander of Kodim 0824 Jember, the region was rocked by a series of riots stemming from land disputes and local outrage over gross electoral violations. After one such riot, during which Djasmin was stabbed, the Kodam commander ordered that Djasmin's mouth be "taped shut" to prevent him from talking to the press. Djasmin later reflected: "It's not that I'm afraid for my career, but I am uncomfortable with the Kodam commander who chewed me out the other night...".[17] While he was honored as one of the seven best Kodim commanders in the country, Djasmin did in fact see his career stagnate: still a lieutenant colonel a full twenty-four years after graduating from the military academy, he will be lucky to make colonel by the time he retires.

Taking a hard-line stance or using violence against a recalcitrant population is doubly risky. On the one hand, the military has clearly adopted sterner measures against personnel who violate stated codes of conduct. This has become particularly apparent after the sacking of several generals held responsible for the 1991 massacre at the Santa Cruz cemetery in Dili, East Timor.[18] On the other hand, by using force against protesters, officers risk alienating precisely those people —civilian leaders and the local population —on whom their future may depend. For with

---

possible for Kodim and battalion commanders. Given the greater number of positions involved, we suspect that there is in fact little difference in relative class success at these levels.

17 See "Komandan Kodim 0824 Jember Diserahterimakan: 'Pangdam Pernah Suruh Mulut Saya Diplester'," *Surabaya Post*, September 9, 1997.

18 The Editors, "Current Data on the Indonesian Military Elite: July 1, 1989-January 1, 1992," *Indonesia* 53 (April 1992): 93-136.

the deterioration of career prospects, the best that most middle-ranking officers can hope for is to be assigned to civilian duty as *bupati* or *walikota*, legislative member, or other civilian functionary. These assignments are most commonly located in the same area where the officer spent the final years of his career.[19] Military leaders frequently note that these assignments are given to officers who have demonstrated an ability to work with —not against —the bureaucracy. The same logic may also hold for officers who do not harbor ambitions to become local officials, since those who have children in public school or who desire to develop business-contacts may find that aggressive moves to repress widespread civilian discontent could make them social outcasts.

There is scattered evidence that over the past several years local military commanders have adopted a far more passive stance towards the growing wave of protest.[20] This is not to deny that incidents of harsh repression continue to occur, but to note that there are numerous instances in which local commanders have adopted a more accommodating approach. They may do so neither out of altruism nor a desire to see a change in the political status quo, but simply to safeguard their own futures.

DINAS KARYA

We need to fill the legislative positions allotted to the ABRI faction, and for that we need people who are still on active duty. Well now, how many will that take? At the center, in the regions, level I and level II. Count for yourself.

    - Army Chief of Staff General Rudini, 1985[21]

At the time of the 1985 Army reorganization, there was considerable

---

19 Malley rightly notes that "candidates for district executive should be selected from among military officers...who have served in that district's province." Michael Malley, "Who is Running the Regions? Regional Political Leadership in Indonesia, 1966-1996," paper presented at the 49th Annual Meeting of the Association for Asian Studies, Chicago, March 13-16, 1997, p. 15.

20 This claim is based on consideration of military responses to popular protest as well as discussions with activists in second-tier cities throughout Java and Bali. Similar observations are made by the LIPI report; see, M. Hamdan Basyar and Sri Yanuarti, "Peran Sosial Politik ABRI Pada Masa Orde Baru," in *Peran Sospol ABRI: Masalah dan Prospeknya*, ed. Indria Samego (unpublished report, Pusat Penelitian dan Pengembangan Politik dan Kewilayahan-LIPI, 1997), p. 82.

21 "Sesudah Saya Jelaskan, Keresahan itu Hilang," *Tempo*, May 4, 1985.

uneasiness within the officer corps about future employment. Army officers were concerned that the streamlining of the Army's territorial commands would result in a reduction in the number of positions available, create stiffer competition for assignments, and ultimately lead to forced retirement of superfluous officers.[22] This in turn created concern within the civil bureaucracy that Army personnel forced to retire would be given civilian posts, perhaps with an overall increase in civil positions held by ABRI. The ensuing discussion offers insight into problems faced by the military leadership at the time and the possibility that similar problems will arise in the future.

To assuage these concerns within the officer corps in 1985, Army Chief of Staff General Rudini offered an extensive explanation of official policy. Rudini chided officers who childishly calculated that the elimination of six Kodams, each commanded by a brigadier general and staffed by six colonels, would result in the loss of positions for six generals and thirty-six colonels. Without providing details, he maintained that such thinking failed to account for massive retirements due to take place that year,[23] concluding that "there would not be any unemployment."[24]

A week later, Rudini offered an extensive explanation about *dwifungsi* after the Army reorganization was completed. Curiously, he noted that ABRI members who sit on the national and local legislatures (DPR and DPRD) were in fact not *dikaryakan* (meaning seconded to civilian duty and therefore no longer active) but rather still on active duty.[25] The new policy, he explained, would stress *dwifungsi* within the course of officers' careers, with officers moving from active duty to *kekaryaan* positions and back again. Career advancement would depend on successful service in both active military and *kekaryaan* positions. Rudini explained that successful service in a *kekaryaan* position would pave the way for a subsequent promotion to a higher ranking appointment in active service,

---

22 This was reminiscent of the concerns which arose following the recommendations of the 1956 Gatot Commission and the resulting reorganization of the army. See Ruth McVey, "The Post-Revolutionary Transformation of the Indonesian Army," Part II, *Indonesia* 13 (April 1972): 154.

23 These presumably involved members of the *Angkatan '45* (1945 Generation) that fought in the revolution and whose numbers had bloated the army officer corps for some time. Indeed, it was in large part the passing of this generation (in terms of both numbers and influence) that facilitated Moerdani's 1983-85 military reorganization.

24 "Sesudah Saya Jelaskan, Keresahan itu Hilang," *Tempo*, May 4, 1985, p. 14.

25 This is referred to as either *kekaryaan* or *dinas karya*, and we use the two terms interchangeably.

but that an otherwise accomplished military officer whose *kekaryaan* service was found wanting would not be promoted. To ensure the smooth rotation of officers between active and *kekaryaan* positions and to ensure acceptance of these policies within the officer corps, Rudini stressed that *kekaryaan* service should not exceed one term at a time.[26]

Rudini went on to explain, however, that he did not have enough active-duty officers to replace all ABRI personnel then serving *kekaryaan* duty. The article notes a curious misunderstanding that arose concerning the number of ABRI personnel sitting on legislatures who needed to be replaced. Rudini is reported to have first said that 70 percent of all ABRI personnel on *kekaryaan* duty needed to be replaced because they were retired. He later clarified this, saying that it only applied to those on the national legislature (DPR RI), and noted that at most he only had the manpower to replace 40 percent of the total. On the basis of this, the *Tempo* article concluded that "in the future the number of ABRI personnel assigned to *kekaryaan* duty as governors, *bupati*, and ministerial staff would be reduced."[27]

But were these policies concerning *kekaryaan* service implemented? Did the overall number of military personnel holding administrative posts decrease? Over the course of the past decade, it appears that military practice has not in fact followed the policies laid out by Rudini. As was the case during the late 1950s and early 1960s, it is virtually unheard of for an officer to move from *kekaryaan* duty back to active military service. The appointment from active military service to a *kekaryaan* position is irreversible.[28] Moreover, there has not been a noticeable change in the number of governorships or *bupati*-ships held by ABRI. Although the percentage of bupati from the military did fall marginally from 50 percent to 41 percent during Rudini's tenure as Interior Minister in the late 1980s, the figure has remained largely unchanged since then,

---

26 "Dwifungsi setelah Reorganisasi" *Tempo*, May 11, 1985, p. 13.

27 Ibid.

28 Compare this to MacFarling's claim that "the most likely [career] path is a criss-cross between duties in the territorial branch of the defence function and the public sector branch of the social-political function." He fails to provide evidence to support the claim, and his figure showing possible career paths is seriously flawed. See Ian MacFarling, *The Dual Function of the Indonesian Armed Forces: Military Politics in Indonesia* (Sydney: Australian Defence Studies Centre, The University of New South Wales, 1996), pp. 148-149.

standing at 44 percent in 1996.[29] Finally, contrary to Rudini's intentions, it is in fact quite common for military personnel on *kekaryaan* duty to serve more than one five-year term.[30]

Unfortunately, there is little information available on the total number of military personnel on *kekaryaan* duty.[31] The officers selected for civilian postings (both commissioned and non-commissioned) are required to attend a two-month course, Kursus Karyawan ABRI, held at the Armed Forces Staff and Command School (Sesko ABRI) in Bandung. During the closing ceremony of each course the Commander-in-Chief of the Armed Forces often notes the number of personnel involved in *kekaryaan* duties. In 1984-85 there were 14,819 members of the Armed Forces serving in *kekaryaan* positions, the total rising to 15,680 by December 1987.[32] No reliable figures are available for the 1990s,[33] though we suspect that the total has continued to rise as the larger classes have reached retirement age or been pushed out of active service.

The 1990s saw increasing debate about *dinas karya*. One issue concerned the rank required for military personnel seconded to the civilian bureaucracy and executive posts. There were repeated suggestions that in the future the requirement for becoming a *bupati* or *walikota*

---

29 See The Editors, "Current Data on the Indonesian Military: July 1, 1989-January 1, 1992," p. 97, and "Tak ada jatah ABRI atau sipil dalam jabatan Kepala Daerah," *Angkatan Bersenjata*, May 29, 1996.

30 For example, 50 percent of all ABRI members of level I and II legislatures (DPRD Tingkat I and II) in Central Java and Yogyakarta were granted a second term. See "ABRI karyakan 396 Personil di DPRD Se-Jateng dan DIY," *Jawa Pos*, June 28, 1997. The article notes that the majority of these officers are "still young," suggesting that they are being removed from active service at a younger age than their predecessors. Similarly, Malley found "a sharp increase during 1993-97 in the proportion of district executives appointed to a second term." See Michael Malley, "Who is Running the Regions?," p. 12.

31 Official Dephankam (Department Hankam) publications on *kekaryaan* are limited to overviews of the ideological, practical, and procedural basis of *kekaryaan*. See for example, Departemen Pertahanan Keamanan, *Tanya-Jawab Dwi Fungsi dan Kekaryaan ABRI* (Jakarta: Ssospol Hankam, 1979), and Departemen Pertahanan Keamanan, *Dwi Fungsi dan Kekaryaan ABRI* (Jakarta: Ssospol Hankam, 1979).

32 "Amanat Panglima ABRI pada Acara pertemuan dengan Pakokar dan Karyawan ABRI Eselon-1 di Markas Besar ABRI Tanggal 15 Juli 1988," *Mimbar Kekaryaan*, July 1988, no. 211, pp. 41-47.

33 Based on interviews, MacFarling believes that in 1992 "there were approximately 14,000 ABRI officers involved in kakaryawan tasks." *The Dual Function of the Indonesian Armed Forces*, p. 145. The authors of the LIPI report, however, claim that the total numbers involved in *kekaryaan* duties has increased throughout the New Order. See M. Hamdan Basyar and Sri Yanuarti, "Peran Sosial Politik ABRI Pada Masa Orde Baru," in *Peran Sospol ABRI*, p. 75.

be raised from colonel to brigadier general.[34] These suggestions were vigorously opposed by the military elite out of concern that the military would lose (or be threatened with the loss of) its best officers to civilian administrative posts.[35] This, however, is not the entire story. Rather, as more and more officers are assigned to *kekaryaan* duty without seeing their military ambitions fulfilled, there were demands to grant higher ranks as a form of appeasement.

A more serious issue relating to *dinas karya* concerns the allocation of legislative seats to the military. In 1995, President Soeharto issued a surprising announcement that the number of seats on the national legislature (DPR/MPR RI) allocated to the military would be reduced by 25 percent from one hundred to seventy-five.[36] Since then, there have been scattered comments about extending this reduction in the size of the ABRI faction at the provincial (DPRD Tingkat I) and district (DPRD Tingkat II) levels. If such a policy were to be adopted, it would involve a 25 percent decrease in the number of legislative *kekaryaan* positions available to the military (approximately 2,800 seats), hitting hard at the large numbers of officers now approaching retirement age. One suspects that such a move would trigger serious resistance from the increasing number of officers reaching mandatory retirement, for whom these positions represent a source of both social standing and financial reward.

During a two-day discussion between current military leaders and a number of retired generals at Sesko ABRI in late 1996, retired General Rudini stirred debate over the military's dual function. "It isn't true that ABRI's *Dwi Fungsi* would be incomplete without *kekaryaan* duty. *Kekaryaan* duty is only one part of *Dwi Fungsi*. Even without *kekaryaan*, there would still be *Dwi Fungsi*." Rudini went on to note that the continuation of *dwifungsi* did not require that ABRI members serve as governors or *bupati*, explaining: "If in all of Indonesia there wasn't a member of ABRI serving as governor or *bupati*, that wouldn't be a

---

34 See "Menpan TB Silalahi: Bupai Harus Berpangkat Brigjen," *Kedaulatan Rakyat*, October 28, 1994, and "Saifullah: Belum Dapat Restu dari Mabes ABRI," *Pikiran Rakyat*, November 22, 1997.

35 See "Pangab Tak Rela Brigjen Jadi Bupati," *Bernas*, November 3, 1994.

36 See, for example, "ABRI: Redefinisi, Bukan ke Tangsi," *Tiras*, March 13, 1997, p. 85. For the most far-reaching proposal, see the comments by former Kostrad Commander Kemal Idris, in "Idealnya di DPR Cukup 30 Orang," *Jawa Pos*, October 12, 1997.

problem. *Dwi Fungsi* isn't determined by *kekaryaan* duty."[37] Discussion of *dwifungsi* and *kekaryaan* continued in April 1997, on the eve of the national elections. Others have echoed this theme. On the occasion of a reunion of graduates of the Army Staff and Command School (Seskoad) in Bandung, the ABRI Assistant for Social and Political Affairs (Assospol Kassospol) Major General Budi Harsono speculated that in the future *kekaryaan* would be reduced in stages. "I must remind you that *kekaryaan* is only one part of the implementation of ABRI's broad social and political role. Most people only view ABRI's socio-political role in its practical manifestations, such as *kekaryaan*."[38]

Considering the thoroughness and ease with which Moerdani's 1983-85 reorganization of the military was conducted, one wonders why the accompanying policies for *kekaryaan* service outlined by Rudini were not implemented as well. The answer, we believe, does not lie in personal conflicts or political factionalism. Rather, the reason is essentially structural: faced with pressures resulting from the changing size of the officer corps, military leaders have been forced to abandon the policies outlined by Rudini so as to provide employment for the excess number of Army personnel. To do otherwise would be to risk dissatisfaction —and perhaps an outright challenge —from within ABRI itself.

RETIREMENT

> It shouldn't be assumed that relations between the retired officer corps and ABRI aren't warm. That's very subjective. I for one don't know what warm relations really means.
> - Syarwan Hamid, Chief of ABRI's Social and Political Staff, 1996[39]

With the completion of the July 1997 wave of personnel changes, the large AMN classes of the mid- to late-1960s are reaching mandatory retirement age. All members of Class 6 (1965) have now been retired from active service, and with the exception of a few officers who made general

---

37 "Penerapan Dwi Fungsi Tidak Ada Masalah," *Pikiran Rakyat*, November 5, 1996.
38 "Usul Mantan Jenderal Jadi Referensi ABRI," *Suara Merdeka*, April 23, 1997.
39 "Penilaian ABRI-Purnawirawan Terlalu Subyektif," *Media Indonesia*, July 23, 1996.

rank, the same is true for most members of the other military academy classes of the late 1960s. The recent announcements of appointments to local legislative bodies reveal that many of these officers are members of classes 10 (1970) through 12 (1972). Whether or not military officers on *kekaryaan* duty are officially retired or still active, there can be no doubt that the size of the retired officer corps has in fact increased sharply over the past several years. This development raises its own questions about military politics in the near future.

The military's most pressing concern remains that of guaranteeing satisfactory employment and business opportunities for these personnel. But while the number of retired officers is now increasing, ABRI finds itself less and less able to provide the benefits that it once did. As we have argued, there has not been a significant change in the number of *kekaryaan* positions allocated to ABRI over the past decade. Similarly, ABRI's business interests, though still extensive, are not as widespread or as lucrative as they once were.[40] Aside from the large foundations (*Yayasan*) associated with the four service branches, ABRI's most important business interests are in real estate, transportation, and, of course, "security" for the private sector.[41] Additionally, the growing ranks of new businesses which have developed during the 1980s are less and less willing, and indeed have less and less need, to place members of the military on their boards of directors to help secure permits and to provide political protection.

With officers' career ambitions often unfulfilled, their opportunities for civilian duty limited, and their expectations thwarted by a military unable to provide other means of employment and remuneration, it comes as little surprise to find growing dissatisfaction among the retired officer corps.[42]

---

40 See, for example, Harold Crouch, *The Army and Politics in Indonesia* (Ithaca, NY: Cornell University Press, 1988) especially chapter eleven, "The Army's Economic Interests."

41 One response has been to encourage retired members of the military to go into the private sector on their own. ABRI has recently instituted a business training program for middle-ranking officers due for retirement. See, "100 Pamen Dididik Jadi Konglomerat," *Merdeka*, May 23, 1996. Lowry claims that "in their last two years, members [of the armed forces] are usually posted to the area where they want to retire and given the time and opportunity to find and establish a civilian career." See Robert Lowry, *The Armed Forces of Indonesia* (St. Leonards: Allen & Unwin, 1996), p. 129. We have not found any evidence that this is true for commissioned officers, though interviews do confirm that it is the case for non-commissioned officers.

42 One of the many recent examples involved a protest by three hundred retired military personnel and civil servants in Ambon to demand payment of pensions. See "Protes 300 Pensiunan," *Kompas*, January 6, 1998.

In itself, of course, criticism from retired military personnel is not new. During the late 1970s, a group of prominent, retired military personnel distressed about President Soeharto's increasingly personalistic rule and the New Order's refusal to allow more democratic practices helped form the *Petisi 50*, or Petition of 50.[43] While a number of the officers involved in *Petisi 50* remained outspoken, the regime successfully managed to silence or deflect much of the criticism, and the group was generally viewed as little more than a few grumpy old men.

During the past several years, however, criticism from within the ranks of the retired officer corps has taken on new dimensions and, with the inevitability of Presidential succession looming ahead, a new relevance. On July 1, 1996, several retired generals led by Lieutenant General Bambang Triantoro and Lieutenant General Kharis Suhud issued a "July 1 Statement of Concern." The content: concern about the current social and political situation in the country.[44] The "July 1 Statement of Concern" was followed by further statements by former Army Commander-in-Chief and Interior Minister Rudini. Rudini is reported to have "insinuated" that relations between ABRI and the retired officer corps had become "unstable" (*kurang mantap*) and "not warm" (*kurang mesra*). According to Rudini, "[r]etired officers always keep abreast of current developments, you know, so they are aware of what's going on. Sometimes they see that policies aren't quite right."[45] Lieutenant General Syarwan Hamid, ABRI's Chief of the Social and Political Staff, was quick to rebut these charges, denying that relations between active and retired officers were "not warm" and judging Rudini's statements to be "overly subjective."[46]

In August 1996 the chairman of Pepabri (Persatuan Purnawirawan ABRI; Association of Retired Members of the Armed Forces of the Republic of Indonesia), Soesilo Soedarman explained that Pepabri would investigate the background of officers considered to be critical of the military and its socio-political role. He was equally quick to distance

---

43 See David Jenkins, *Suharto and his Generals: Indonesian Military Politics 1975-1983* (Ithaca, NY: Cornell Modern Indonesia Project, 1984).

44 See "Sekadar Kangen-kangen Para Bintang," *Tiras*, April 24, 1997, pp. 12-14; "Penilaian ABRI-Purnawirawan Terlalu Subyektif," *Media Indonesia*, July 23, 1996; and the interview with Bambang Triantoro in "Ia Takut Melanggar Sumpah," *Gatra*, December 21, 1996.

45 Ibid.

46 Ibid.

himself from responsibility for the problem, however, noting that "Pepabri isn't responsible for the attitudes of retired officers who are not members of the organization."[47] A month later, Pepabri held its second central meeting, Rakerpus II Pepabri, stimulating a new outpouring of comments and controversy. In an interview the day before the meeting, Lieutenant General (ret.) Solichin GP, former secretary of the watchdog agency Sekdalopbang (Secretariat for Operational Control and Development), issued a statement that the recent flurry of criticism from retired officers was "intended to be constructive." He remarked:

> As for the former generals who are accused of being insubordinate [*mbalelo*] and are said to want to change the system by violence, confrontation, and revolution. Well, there aren't any. There aren't any. Its tough enough for them to recover from being sick, they're all old now.[48]

At the Pepabri meeting on September 25, Soesilo acknowledged that there were some retired officers who made statements and behaved in a manner not "consistent" with Pepabri. He called for all retired members of ABRI to join Pepabri: "In addition to screening new members, this policy will also prevent the possibility of retired officers crossing the fence [going into opposition]."[49] Although no explanation was given, the notion of "crossing over the fence" echoed General Try Sutrisno's statements during the 1992 election about retired officers betraying the military and the state by secretly "crossing over" to support the oppositional Indonesian Democratic Party (PDI).

Despite Pepabri's efforts to suppress its wayward officers and restore a facade of unity among the retired corps, criticism and challenges continued to surface. In January 1997, retired Major General Soebijakto, formerly Governor of the National Defense Institute (Lemhanas), called

---

47 "Pak Sus: Aspirasi Pepabri ke Golkar" *Jawa Pos*, August 7, 1996.

48 "Sikap Kritis Semata-mata Membantu," *Kompas*, September 25, 1996. In this, he was probably echoing comments reportedly made by President Soeharto: "...they are just a small group of people, and one day their time will run out."

49 "Ada Purnawirawan yang tidak konsisten," *Media Indonesia*, September 26, 1996, and "Di Depan Presiden Soeharto: Soesilo Akui Ada Purnawirawan Kurang Konsisten," *Republika*, September 26, 1996.

for the Army to hold a seminar on strategy. In calling for a full-scale discussion of the military's position along the lines of the seminar held at the Army Staff and Command School in August 1966, Soebijakto was inviting a full reappraisal of the political status quo.[50]

In April, the Army Staff and Command School held a reunion for graduates from the 1951-61 period (at which time the school was known by the initials SSKAD). Although a number of generals known for being "critical" of current military policy and the regime were invited, the most vocal were excluded by limiting the event to 1951-61 graduates.[51] Not one to miss an opportunity, General Rudini, who was not invited, again fanned the flames by making public statements about the frequent misunderstandings between the military and the retired officer corps.[52]

But perhaps the most notable challenge from retired officers came during the four-week official campaign period. Speaking about the "White Group" (*Golongan Putih*, abbreviated Golput), a campaign to protest the May national elections, General (Ret.) Theo Syafei,[53] a member of the national legislature (DPR RI), offered this blunt assessment:

> Golput isn't the same as a boycott, so it's perfectly legitimate. If we enter the voting booth and then punch the ballot for all three party lists, that's a protest, and protest is the right of citizens who do not have a real choice.[54]

---

50 "Strategi dan Sasaran Baru Perlu Segera Dirumuskan," *Kompas*, January 13, 1997. The following week, Soebijakto died.

51 There are rumors that other "critical" voices refused to attend what they viewed as a "leisurely" event that offered no opportunity for serious dialogue with the current military leadership.

52 See "Rudini: ABRI-Purnawirawan Sering Terjadi Salah Paham," *Media Indonesia*, April 10, 1997, and "KSAD pada Pembukaan SSKAD Tidak ada 'Gap' antar-Jenderal," *Media Indonesia*, April 12, 1997.

53 A Butonese Christian, Theo graduated from the AMN in 1965, and served in many capacities in the East Timor campaign. During the last ten years he has served as: Commander of Korem 081 Madiun (1987-88); Chief of Staff of the Kostrad Second Infantry Division (1988-89); commander of the Kostrad Second Infantry Division (1989-91); Chief of Staff of Kodam II Sriwijaya (1991-92); Commander of the Operational Command (Kolakops) in East Timor (1992-93); and Commander of Kodam IX Udayana (1993-94). He was then assigned to a seat on the national legislature (DPR RI).

54 It is worth providing this remarkable statement in its original Indonesian: "Golput itu sahsah saja, sebab tidak sama dengan boikot pemilu. Kalau kita masuk ke bilik kemudian mencoblos ketiga-tiganya, itu merupakan sikap protes, karena itu hak sebagai warga negara yang tidak mempunyai pilihan." Quoted in "Giliran Theo di 'Recall'," *Forum Keadilan*, June 2, 1996.

Public acknowledgment of Golput and the frank assessment that the national elections did not offer a choice were clearly more than either the military elite or President Soeharto could tolerate. Shortly thereafter, Theo was unceremoniously "recalled" from his position as a member of the national legislature.[55]

Extensive as these statements and debates were, one must recall that they were essentially limited to members of the military elite. All of the participants involved were generals each with one or more star to his name. But dissent within the retired officer corps is not limited to generals. Indeed, the analysis developed in the preceding sections suggests that there may be serious dissatisfaction within the large cohort of officers who graduated from the military academy during the late 1960s and early 1970s and who are now reaching mandatory retirement. While each of these classes does have its champions, the vast majority of these officers did not have the opportunity to rise beyond the rank of lieutenant colonel or colonel; given their greater numbers, there are simply not enough *kekaryaan* positions to go around; and, because of the economic crisis that began in mid-1997, the military is no longer capable of providing the post-retirement benefits that it once did. Again, it is necessary to emphasize that the impact of these shrinking opportunities is not limited in its effect to a small group; rather, the importance of the trend lies precisely in the extremely large number of officers involved.

This is not to suggest the likelihood of an open mutiny on the part of retired officers. But there is every reason to believe such dissatisfaction will make this large contingent of officers more willing to contemplate genuine political change. Nor is this to suggest that retired officers have a meaningful voice in the military's decisionmaking or policy formation. They do not. Instead, we are arguing that among the growing numbers of disgruntled and frustrated retired officers, there may be some who prove willing to support calls for political reform. This is precisely what happened in May 1998 at the time of the massive national demonstrations demanding Soeharto's resignation and both political and economic reform. A number of retired officers joined the chorus calling for a special session

---

55 Ibid. He was not formally replaced until August. See "Mayjen TNI Theo Syafei resmi ditarik dari DPR," *Angkatan Bersenjata*, August 21, 1997.

of the People's Consultative Council and for Soeharto to be replaced.[56] We fully expect to see further instances of this in the near future and for it to extend well below the ranks of retired generals to include the much larger numbers of colonels and lieutenant colonels whose careers never lived up to youthful (though perhaps unrealistic) ambitions.

THE POST-1975 REVERSAL

> The younger officers are much more liberal and open than the older generation...At least when you talk to them you are not scared.
> - Nasir Tamara, member of the Indonesian Association of Muslim Intellectuals, 1993[57]

Thus far we have limited our analysis to the implications that the sharp increase in academy graduates during the 1960s and early 1970s had on the officer corps and the means by which the Army leadership responded to these challenges. Beginning in 1975-76, however, a sharp reversal took place, with the number of cadets graduating from the renamed Akabri plummeting below one hundred and remaining at this low level through 1983 (see Table 1.1). The institutional implications of this reversal, which oppose and thus mirror the implications of the preceding analysis, can be analyzed briefly.

Whereas larger class size at the military academy made for poorer career prospects, the small size of the post-1975 classes dramatically improves the promotional prospects for this younger generation of officers. This is most clearly and dramatically illustrated by the age at which officers are posted as Kodim commanders. The mean age for the large Akabri classes 10 (1970) through 14 (1974) was forty-one years at time of appointment to Kodim command; by contrast the mean age for the much smaller classes 15 (1975) through 18 (1978) is thirty-seven years. Recalling the discussion of the data in Table 3.1, it seems likely that 15-20 percent of the officers in each class will become Korem commanders, with as many as 5 to 10 percent becoming Kodam commanders. Even more remarkable,

---

56 See, for example, "General Purnawirawan anggap perlu SI MPR," *Waspada*, May 16, 1998.
57 Quoted in Adam Schwarz, *A Nation in Waiting: Indonesia in the 1990s* (Boulder: Westview Press, 1994), p. 289.

almost all of the weapons officers (i.e. infantry, artillery, etc.) from these classes can look forward to reaching the general rank.

It remains to be seen what effect this change in promotional prospects will have on the political outlook of these officers. On the one hand, it could be argued that with extraordinary career prospects, these officers will recognize that all they need do is maintain a clean record and their advancement to the rank of general is all but assured. In this light, we might expect heightened professionalism or, at the least, greater attention to military rules and regulations. On the other hand, with the military finding itself short of commissioned officers at particular ranks, the reduced size of these classes from the military academy might also be accompanied by an increase in the tenure of staff and command officers. This, in turn, might provide opportunities for officers to develop greater regional interests, as was the case during the rebellious 1950s.

In the long term, this reduction in the size of the officer corps should also ease pressure for *kekaryaan* positions. This, of course, will come as welcome news to the large civilian bureaucracy, among which there has long been hope that appointments will be based on performance and professionalism only, and that the predetermined *jatah* (share) set aside for military personnel would be phased out. In this context, it is worth considering the recent view of National Defence Institute Deputy Governor Dr. Juwono Sudarsono, who has argued that "there will be a natural reduction in ABRI's *dwifungsi*" as professional and technical skills in the bureaucracy and private sector increase.[58] Juwono may be correct, but such a reduction in *dwifungsi* may take place for even more "natural" reasons: a simple reduction (or even shortage) of manpower in the Army. Short of manpower, the Army in particular and the Armed Forces high command in general may find that they have a reduced capacity to fill positions in the civilian bureaucracy.

CONCLUSION

For some time now, observers of the Indonesian military have claimed that

---

58 See "Dr. Juwono: Secara Alami Kadar Dwifungsi ABRI Akan Berkurang," *Suara Pembaruan*, March 12, 1997.

there are serious divisions within the Army elite. The editors of *Indonesia* highlighted the efforts of factions within the military elite to remove officers contaminated by their association with Benny Moerdani. Others underlined the tensions between Army professionals and officers who have risen through personal connections to the palace. More recently, gossip in Jakarta focused on the personal rivalry between Kostrad Commander Lieutenant General Prabowo and ABRI Commander-in-Chief General Wiranto. Real as these divisions may have been, our analysis suggests that this focus on individual personalities may inadvertently over-politicize analyses of the workings of the Indonesian Army. Indeed, as this is being written, one cannot help but be struck by the unity within the Indonesian military in a time of crisis. There have no doubt been serious abuses by the security forces, but the military in general, and the Army in particular, has remained institutionally united.

This is not to deny that there are divisions or conflicts within the Indonesian Army. In contrast to analyses which focus on individual personalities, our work has highlighted structural fault lines between the active and retired Army officers.[59] It is not the possibility of being posted in hell that is of such great concern to Army officers, but rather the possibility that one might not be transferred out again after a standard two-year tour of duty. And it is not so much a question of an undesirable posting that haunts the post-retirement fantasies of Army officers, as it is a fear that one might not be posted to a *kekaryaan* position at all.

---

59 It is important to emphasize that, although structurally parallel, this argument is fundamentally distinct from MacFarling's claims about a division between the active and retired officer corps. MacFarling argues that there is "a rift between the serving members of ABRI and the members of *Angkatan 45* and retirees." See MacFarling, *The Dual Function of the Indonesian Armed Forces*, p. 169. Our argument, by contrast, highlights divisions within the generation(s) that graduated from the National Military Academy in Magelang between, say, 1960 and 1984.

CONCLUSION

Two themes dominated discussion of Indonesian politics over the past decade —presidential succession and democratization. While some observers believed that democratic actors would influence the outcome of political succession, the causal link was normally drawn in the other direction. Most scholars argued that meaningful democratization would only become possible in a post-Soeharto Indonesia. In the words of one author: "the inevitable transition from Soeharto...poses the best opportunity for greater democratization because the new President may do well to think about democratization as a means of securing new legitimacy for himself."[1] Others, like William Liddle, were far less sanguine about the situation:

> The democratic forces poised to exploit such a [political] opening are growing in numbers and resources, but foes of democracy, specifically the active leaders of the army, will at that point control the state...We should not underestimate their will and capacity to maintain the regime or...to intensify its repressive and authoritarian features.[2]

The relationship between political change and the military presents a clear dilemma for progressive forces. In the words of Arief Budiman:

> We know we have to work with Abri [sic] if we are to achieve a transition of power but we are worried that the army will take over

---

1   Chua Beng Huat, "Looking for Democratization in Post-Soeharto Indonesia," *Contemporary Southeast Asia* 15,2 (September 1993): 157.
2   R. William Liddle, "Indonesia's Threefold Crisis," *Journal of Democracy* 3,4 (October 1992): 74.

again once Soeharto is gone…Right now we have a common cause with Abri, just like we did in 1965-66. But can we carve out enough space for ourselves so that Abri won't take it all away once their objective has been reached? This is what they did in the late 1960s and I'm afraid they could do it again. If that is going to happen, what's the point of trying to push out Soeharto?[3]

The extraordinary events of May 1998 and the fall of Soeharto have brought these concerns to the forefront. In one of the most cogent discussions of the succession-democratization dilemma, Adam Schwarz rightly raised a central problem for the civilian elite: "how to identify which segment of Abri might be open to a dialogue. Some argue that the so-called 1945 Generation of Abri officers offers the best hope…Others hope for better things from the younger officers."[4]

Before plunging into the uncharted territory of political developments in the post-Soeharto era, we are well advised to return to the questions and puzzles with which this study began. These were posed in two sets. The first set concerned the development of military politics, particularly the internal dynamics of the Army, during the past decade. Why did large-scale personnel changes accelerate in frequency and broaden in scope during this period? On what basis are personnel decisions in the Army made —not only for the handful of officers at the peak of the military apparatus but for the officer corps as a whole?

A second set of questions is raised by the sudden fall of a man who ruled Indonesia for over thirty-two years. This is not the place for a sociological analysis of the economic crisis, protests, and riots that brought Soeharto down. But it is appropriate to raise questions about how the military responded to the political crisis. Observers of the Indonesian military frequently have noted that Soeharto maintained his grip on power through the appointment to senior military posts of relatives and officers who had served him personally. Why, then, did the military elite not defend Soeharto in his hour of need? Commentators have also argued that the military is deeply divided. How, then, are we to

---

3   Quoted in Adam Schwarz, *A Nation in Waiting: Indonesia in the 1990s* (Boulder: Westview Press, 1994), p. 287.
4   Ibid., p. 288.

explain the apparent unity of the military (with one or two exceptions) in a time of crisis?

Finally, if Arief Budiman and others are correct that the prospects for political change hinge on the behavior and interests of the military, then it is with the military that an analysis of the current political configuration must begin.

RETURN TO MAGELANG

Against existing analyses, we have argued that the waves of personnel reshuffles in the Indonesian military during the mid-1990s are neither simply, nor most fundamentally, the result of current political maneuvering in Jakarta. They are instead a response to two dilemmas —one structural, the other stemming from personnel procedures.

The first of these dilemmas can be traced to Magelang, Central Java three decades ago, and the tremendous increase in the size of classes graduated from the National Military Academy between 1960 and the mid-1970s. The problems of accommodating the ballooning size of the officer corps were exacerbated by a second dilemma stemming from personnel practice: by allowing an officer who completed his tour of duty in a given post to recommend a suitable replacement, the first of the large classes from the military academy gained a virtual monopoly on staff and command positions. It is in light of these twin dilemmas that we must understand the military elite's emphasis on *regenerasi* during the 1990s. The high command responded to this dual challenge by shortening the tenure of staff and command officers from the rank of major through major general. Additional "corrective" measures were also adopted. The total number of officers from each class appointed to key command positions was standardized, ensuring that no one class would gain a monopoly. The variation in command tenure was greatly reduced. And career paths of commissioned Army officers have been standardized, thus stabilizing expectations within the officer corps.

Decreasing tenure was not the only response available to the military elite, of course. The military could have increased the number of billets for commissioned officers. It could have added new educational requirements for promotion and assignment of Army officers, thereby weeding out "excess" personnel. It could have instituted mandatory retirement for officers who failed to make a specified rank by a certain age, a common practice in most modern militaries. Each of these potential remedies carried its own risks. Increasing the number of billets would have upset the streamlining of the military that General Benny Moerdani so carefully planned and carried out during the early 1980s. The adoption of new obstacles to career advancement or mandatory retirement would likely have been viewed as a direct threat to the officer corps and might well have led to outright resistance. The path chosen —decreasing the tenure of staff and command officers —was a politically astute compromise, allowing a greater number of officers the opportunity to serve in key positions with the least degree of obvious dislocation.

Having explored a number of the bureaucratic dynamics at work within the Indonesian Army, our discussion then turned to some of the political implications of these changes. We argued that, while the increased number of commissioned officers has provided the Army with the manpower necessary for greater specialization, it has also presented the Army and Armed Forces high commands with a series of new quandaries. First, shortened tenure of territorial commanders means that these officers will have less knowledge of both their responsibilities and of local dynamics, and therefore will be less well prepared to anticipate and respond to social unrest. Though we are cautious about drawing a direct causal link, the correlation between declining command tenure during the 1990s and the increasing frequency of riots is unmistakable. Second, the greater the size of the officer corps, the worse are the career prospects for individual officers. And as career prospects deteriorated, local command officers found less and less incentive to take strong action against social unrest. A third point concerns the assignment of military officers to *kekaryaan* duty: the greater the size of the officer corps, the more need there will be for lucrative and prestigious assignments after retirement from active duty. Finally, we discussed the growing dissatisfaction among members of the retired officer corps who have seen career ambitions remain unfulfilled and found that the military is both less able and less willing to care for its own after active duty.

THE ARMY AT A CROSSROADS

We can now turn to the second set of questions raised by the events of

May 1998. How are we to explain the behavior of the Indonesian Army in a time of crisis? Why did the military elite, led by officers selected for their personal loyalty to Soeharto, not defend the embattled President? With several tragic exceptions, why did the military refrain from a full-scale and bloody crackdown on either student protesters or the rioters of May 14 and 15? Why, when most commentators have emphasized the divisions within the Armed Forces, has the military in general and the Army in particular remained united?

One might, of course, attempt to answer these questions by appealing to general aspects of the situation. Perhaps the political crisis provided sudden reason for the military to overcome its internal rifts, uniting diverse views and personal ambitions in the face of the greater challenge posed to the military's position in the political system. This sort of reasoning, however, is far from compelling. Alternatively, one might renew the long-standing focus on personalities and argue that a major split within the military was only narrowly averted by General Wiranto's decision on May 22 to transfer Soeharto son-in-law Lieutenant General Prabowo from his post as commander of the Army Strategic Command to head the Armed Forces Staff and Command School (Sesko ABRI) in Bandung.[5] This, however, still fails to account for the failure of the military to defend Soeharto. Nor can such an approach explain the loyalty displayed by the commissioned officer corps to ABRI Commander-in-Chief General Wiranto throughout the crisis.

This monograph has emphasized at least four features that may help to provide answers to these questions. First, our analysis highlighted the precipitous drop in command tenure within the Army officer corps over the past decade. Reduced command tenure and more rapid reassignment during the past several years may have had the unintentional effect of hindering the establishment of regional interests and, more generally, preventing the formation of cliques within the officer corps. In this regard the sudden reassignment of Lieutenant General Prabowo is instructive,

---

5   This face-saving exercise fails to address the very real abuses committed by Prabowo during the preceding months. See "Pangkostrad dan Danjen Kopassus Diganti," *Media Indonesia*, May 23, 1998. The previous day gossip circulated that Wiranto had ordered Prabowo's arrest in connection with the murders of six students during a peaceful demonstration at Trisakti University the week before. "Let-jen [sic] Prabowo Pelaku perintah tembak mahasiswa Triskati," posted on <APAKABAR@clark.net>, May 22, 1998.

for it clearly illustrates that most observers over-estimated his influence within the officer corps and the breadth of his personal following. Often touted for the strength of his support within the officer corps, Prabowo was unceremoniously shunted off to an insignificant post in the provincial capital of West Java with little more than a whimper.

Second, our analysis revealed that a significant process of standardization and regularization has taken place within the Army during the past decade. To the extent that Army officers have stable expectations and believe that the military has an institutional rationale for assignments and promotions, they are less likely to act outside of the chain of command or to be lured into factionalism.

Third, this monograph has argued that an important division within the Indonesian Armed Forces exists between the active and retired officer corps. Specifically, we argued that members of the large classes which graduated from the military academy during the late 1960s and early 1970s fared far less well because of the heightened competition for a limited number of posts. The last days of Soeharto saw a number of retired officers come out in support of the President's resignation and in favor of calls for new elections. This period witnessed vast and widespread opportunism, to be sure, but the actions of retired officers represent quite a different dynamic. Finding their career ambitions unfulfilled and the military less and less able to provide for them financially, some of these officers proved willing to support calls for real political reform.

Fourth, this monograph highlighted the political implications of the changing size of the officer corps for the exceptionally small classes that graduated from the military academy beginning in the late 1970s. Small numbers make for extraordinary career prospects. It therefore should not come as a surprise that members of these small classes would act cautiously, obeying commands and avoiding the use of violence against civilian protesters. For these officers are well aware that they are virtually assured of making the rank of Brigadier General (while on active duty) provided they maintain a clear record, and they know that a high percentage from each class will in fact rise higher still. Career prospects thus provide strong incentive for much of the behavior that we have just witnessed.

Lastly, how will the Army respond to the new political configuration? What effect will the current crisis have on the promotional process and tenure trends? The emergency personnel changes made by General Wiranto in the days following Soeharto's resignation will, as we have already seen in chapter one, further lower the tenure trend for Kodam (and perhaps also Korem) commanders. But while personnel reshuffles continue to take place, it would be a mistake to conclude automatically that all of these represent General Wiranto's ongoing effort to strengthen his own hand. While Wiranto has gained considerable control over the military through the appointment of officers who share a similar vision and commitment to defending the military and its position in the political process, personnel changes will also continue to take place for essentially structural reasons.

Wiranto's own explanations are revealing and, even if disingenuous, bear consideration. When asked about the emergency personnel changes made in the days following Soeharto's resignation, Wiranto explained: "The Army and the Armed Forces of Indonesia are not split. The Army remains compact…" In this he is clearly correct. He went on to explain that the reappointment of Lieutenant Prabowo "was planned long ago, but because national circumstances did not make the transfer possible, it was only done now once the situation had settled down." In this, he was disingenuous. But in one last comment, he underlined a feature that has long been neglected in the study of the Indonesian military: the reassignment of officers, he added, was part of the "normal procedure within the Army to ensure that all officers enjoy the requisite tour of duty."[6]

6 See "Pangab: Sudah Lama Direncanakan," *Suara Merdeka*, May 24, 1998.

THE RELATIONSHIP BETWEEN ABRI LEADERSHIP AND KODAM COMMAND TENURE

The changes in tenure of Kodam commanders during the 1985-1997 period appear to correspond to the leadership of different ABRI commanders in chief (*Panglima ABRI*; Pangab). How and why did this occur? If changes in command tenure correspond to the tenure of different Pangabs, isn't this evidence that these changes occurred for political rather than structural reasons? The somewhat technical nature of our explanation requires that these questions be addressed here in an appendix rather than in the body of the text. This, however, does not lessen the importance of the issues at stake.

Let us first establish the correspondence between Kodam command (Pangdam) tenure and ABRI leadership. The appointment of ABRI commander-in-chief has historically been for the five-year period of the presidency. General Moerdani was appointed Pangab in 1983, carried out the territorial reconfiguration of the Army between 1983-85, and served until early 1988.[1] During this first phase, Pangdam tenure remained stable. General Try Soetrisno served as Pangab from 1988 until February 1993, during which time the tenure of Pangdam first increased and then decreased dramatically. In February 1993 Try Soetrisno was replaced as Pangab by the professional and highly-capable General Edi Sudradjat. Although he only served as Pangab for four months, Edi carried out far-reaching personnel changes. Immediately following the election of

---

1 Moerdani's replacement in February 1988 is remarkable in that it occurred one month prior to the MPR session to elect the President and Vice President, a move intended to deprive the powerful Panglima ABRI of influence over the choice and appointment of Vice President.

President Soeharto to a fifth term in 1993, General Feisal Tanjung was appointed Pangab, a position he held until February 1998, at which time he was appointed Coordinating Minister for Politics and Security (*Menko Polkam*) in the new cabinet. The third phase, from 1993 until 1997, was initiated by Edi Sudradjat and covers the full tenure of General Feisal Tanjung. In Figure 1.1 we see that the tenure of Pangdam passed through three quite distinct phases and note that these phases correspond to the tenure of respective Pangabs. But correspondence does not necessarily mean that there is a causal relationship; that is a separate question.

Are these phases best explained by structural features of the officer corps or by policies and politics associated with the Pangab? The period 1985-1988 was one of generational transition overseen by General Benny Moerdani. During this time Pangdams were taken over by officers who graduated in the first two classes from the AMN. These were small classes, making the career prospects of these officers quite good. During this period, the small number of officers per class made it possible to maintain mean command tenure at a stable level (eight hundred to nine hundred days per officer).

The period 1988-1990, which corresponds to the first half of General Try Sutrisno's tenure as Pangab, saw a modest increase in overall command tenure. The explanation for this does not lie with the appointment of a new Pangab, however, but rather with changes in the officer corps itself. By the late 1980s the pre-AMN generation was being phased out of active duty and was certainly no longer eligible for appointment as Pangdam. Coupled with the relatively small and uniform sizes of the AMN classes in 1961-1963, this meant that there were far fewer officers now eligible for and seeking appointment to these prestigious posts. It was this that allowed Pangdam tenure to increase from 850 to over 1,000 days. Beginning in 1992-1993, however, members of the far larger Class 5 (1964) with 280 officers and Class 6 (1965) with 433 officers were first appointed to serve as Pangdam. Because of the huge size of these classes it was necessary to reduce command tenure in order to allow as many officers as possible to hold these prestigious posts. It was because of this that command tenure plummeted, hitting bottom in 1993 —at exactly the moment that Class 6 (1965) came to monopolize the Pangdamships.

With the brief tenure of General Edi Sudradjat and his replacement by General Feisal Tanjung, we see Pangdam tenure first stabilize at the

540 day level —an extremely short tenure —for the period during which the large Class 6 (1965) monopolized the Pangdamships. In 1995-1996 tenure then increased to around 680 days per commander, this coming at precisely the time that officers from the significantly smaller Class 7 (1966) and Class 8 (1967) were appointed as Pangdams. This, our third phase in command tenure, is in fact a relatively tight band, and reflects both the changes in class size for these graduating classes *and* the need to bring some sort of order to the chaotic changes in Pangdam tenure during the preceding period.

Thus far we have argued that the changing size of the officer corps is the driving force behind these changes in Pangdam tenure; it just so happens that these changes neatly correspond to the tenure of different ABRI commanders-in-chief.

The critical reader might observe that the precipitous drop in Pangdam tenure in mid-1997 occurred under Feisal Tanjung's leadership, and therefore conclude that this undermines our own analysis. Surely this sharp drop in tenure during Feisal's leadership calls into question the periodization that we have employed. Furthermore, this must be a result and reflection of the appointment of a new Pangab and hence of political rather than structural considerations. The explanations for this are worth considering in some detail. Although the decline in Pangdam tenure that began in mid-1997 did occur while Feisal was still Pangab, it in fact reflects changes made in early 1998 by the new Pangab General Wiranto. In August 1997 Feisal appointed a number of new Pangdam who might reasonably have expected to serve for at least six hundred to seven hundred days each. But these officers were then replaced by officers chosen by Feisal's successor, General Wiranto, in the period from April to June 1998. That means that the *mean* tenure for all officers who served from August 1997 onwards was driven down. This is, in essence, a lead effect that is more a product of the statistical method employed than it is a reflection of ABRI leadership at the time that the change appears on our graphs. Looking back several years we can observe that a virtually identical phenomenon occurred in 1992-1993, with personnel changes made by a new Pangab driving down the mean tenure of those officers who served as Pangdam during the end of the previous Pangab's leadership. We are thus seeing a "lead-effect," not a reversal of causal logic. This does not override the structural explanation already provided, but does reveal that the existing structural imbalances caused by the changing size of the officer corps were exacerbated by changes in ABRI leadership at the time of national elections.

This, then, brings us to the second, and in many ways more significant, problem. If it is true that changes in ABRI leadership have had an effect on the appointment and replacement of Pangdam, then must we not concede that these are political, not structural, reasons for the decreases in Pangdam tenure? Here the answer is decidedly mixed. On the one hand, yes: new Pangab have overseen the appointment of new Pangdam. But the reasons for this are essentially *institutional*. First, large-scale personnel changes are traditionally carried out in August, around the time of the national independence day celebrations and before the Armed Forces day celebrations in early October. This means that an outgoing Pangab may make new appointments in August-September, only to see his successor replace these same officers early the following year. Thus a high rate of turn-over in Pangdam need not reflect choices made on the basis of personal loyalty or cliques, as is commonly assumed by observers. Second, completion of the MPR session to select the President also sets in motion the replacement of provincial governors, a significant number of whom are military officers. Furthermore, it has been the practice not only to select officers who are still on active duty, but in fact to appoint officers currently serving as Pangdam to become provincial governors of the same province. Once again, we see that there are institutional reasons for the replacement of Pangdam immediately after the appointment of a new Pangab.

In sum, while we find that there is a close correspondence between Pangabs and the changes in tenure of Kodam commanders, we also argue that this does not entail a direct causal relationship between the two. Rather, the changes in Kodam command tenure are first and foremost a result of and response to the changing size of the officer corps. Furthermore, we have argued that the precipitous drops in Kodam tenure in late 1992-1993 and 1997-1998 are best explained by structural and institutional features of the military and political systems, not by personalities, cliques, and political maneuvering.

Appendix 1.2: Mean Tenure for Korem Commanders: Java vs. Outer Islands
(May 1990 to May 1997)

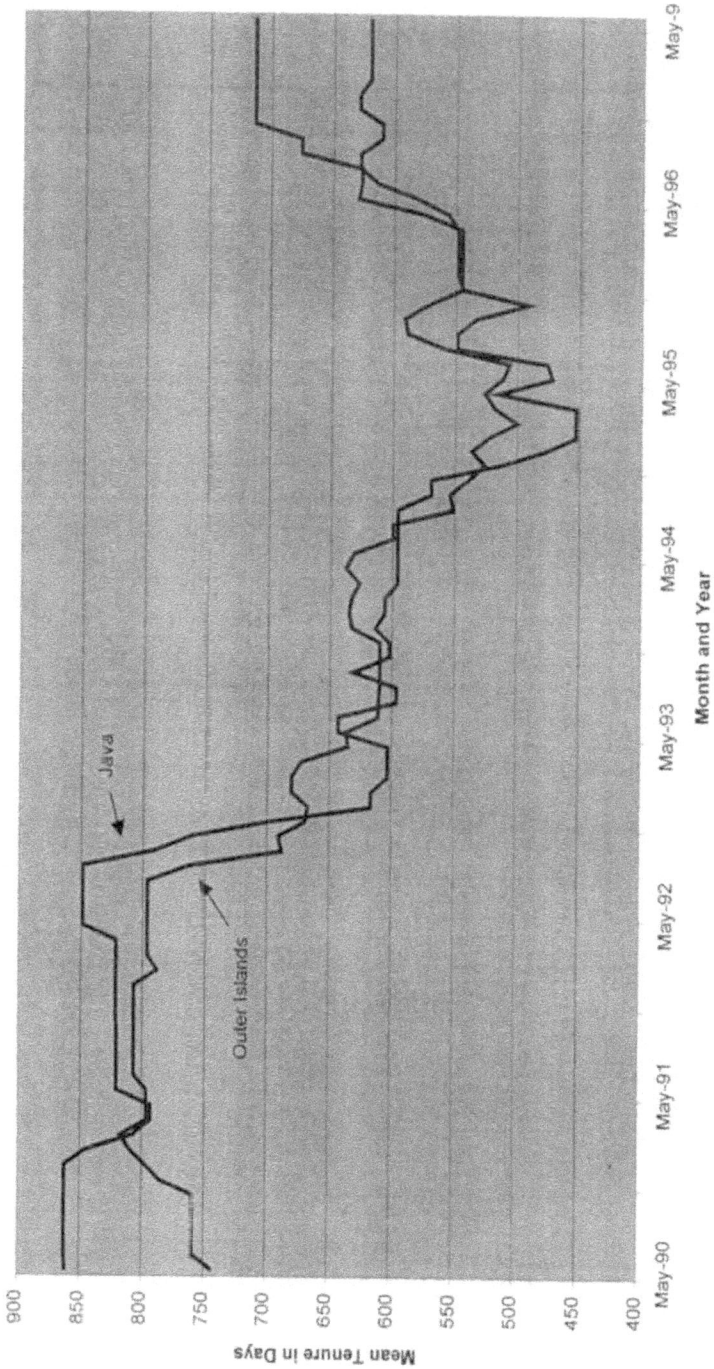

Appendix 1.3: Mean Tenure for Korem Commanders: Trouble/Operations Areas vs. Other Areas
(May 1990 to May 1997)

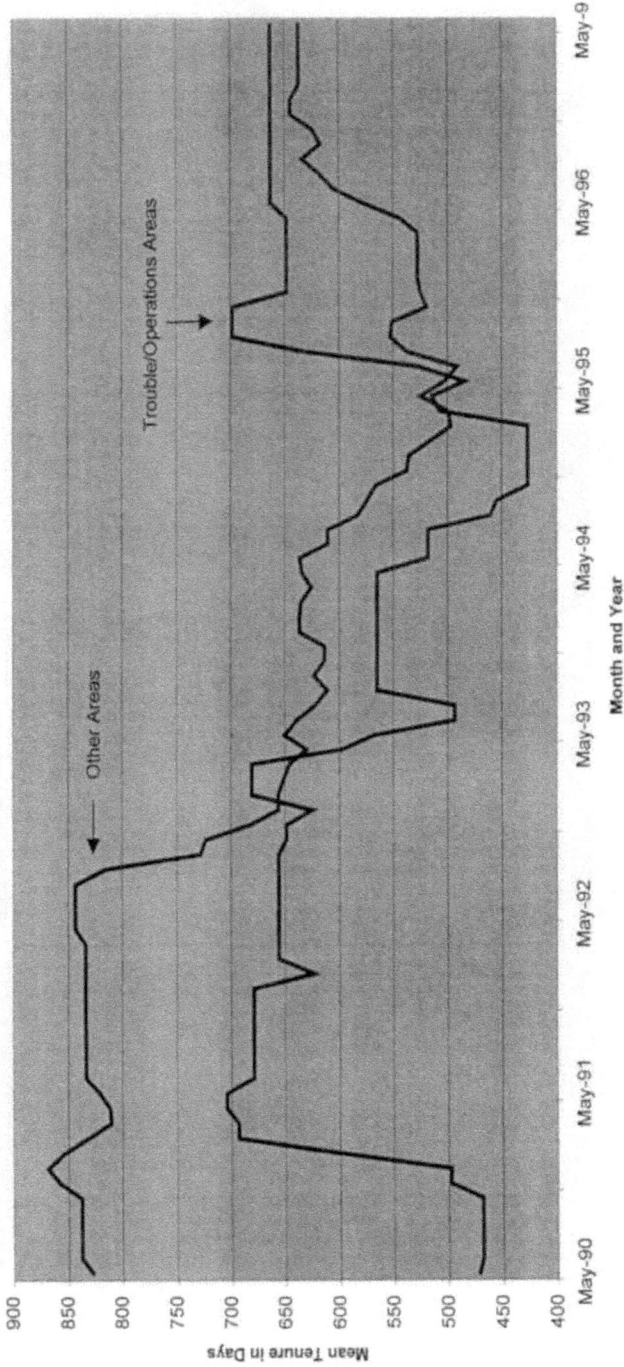

Note: The Trouble/Operations Areas are Korem 011 Liliawangsa (Lhokseumawe), Korem 121 Alambhana Wanawai (West Kalimantan), Korem 164 Wiradharma (East Timor), Korem 171 Praja Vira Tama (Manokwari), Korem 172 Raja Vira Yakthi (Abepura), and Korem 173 PVB (Biak Serui).

Appendix 1.4: Correspondence between Korem and Kodam Command Tenure
(1985-1997)

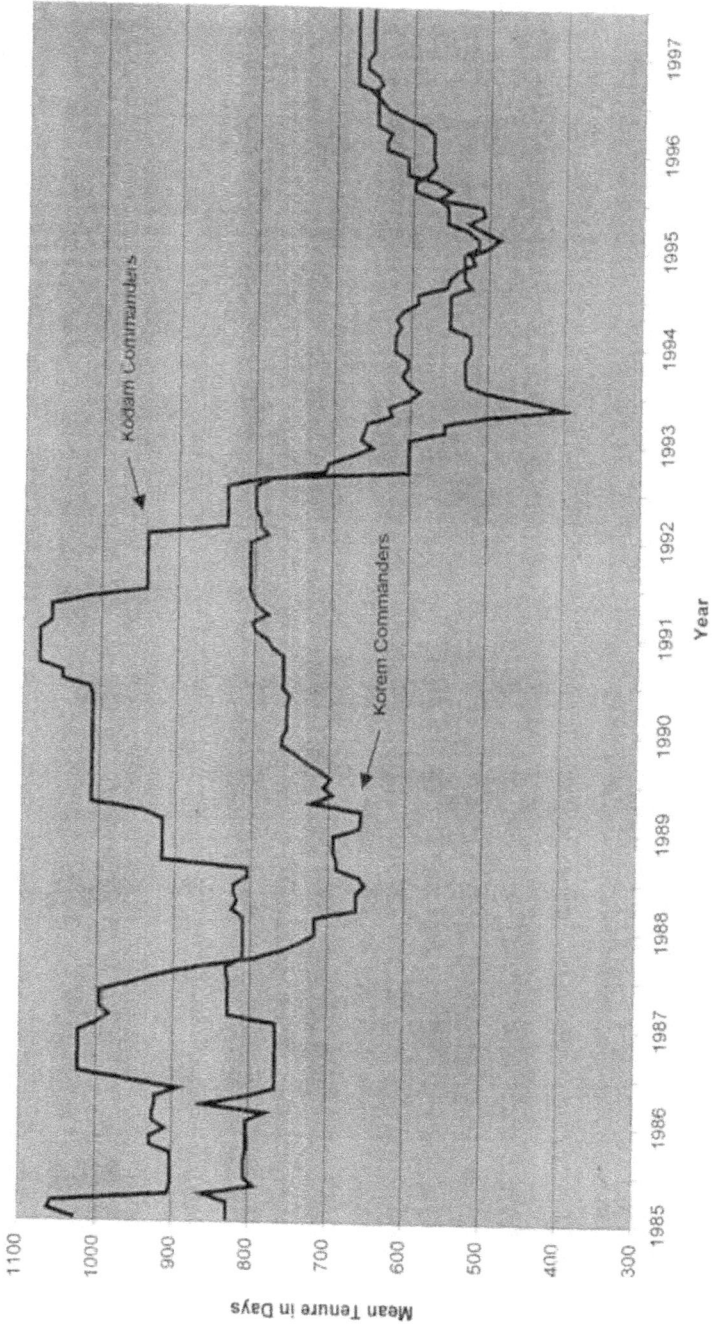

Appendix 1.5: Correspondence between Korem and Kodam Tenure Lagged by Five Years
(1985-1991)

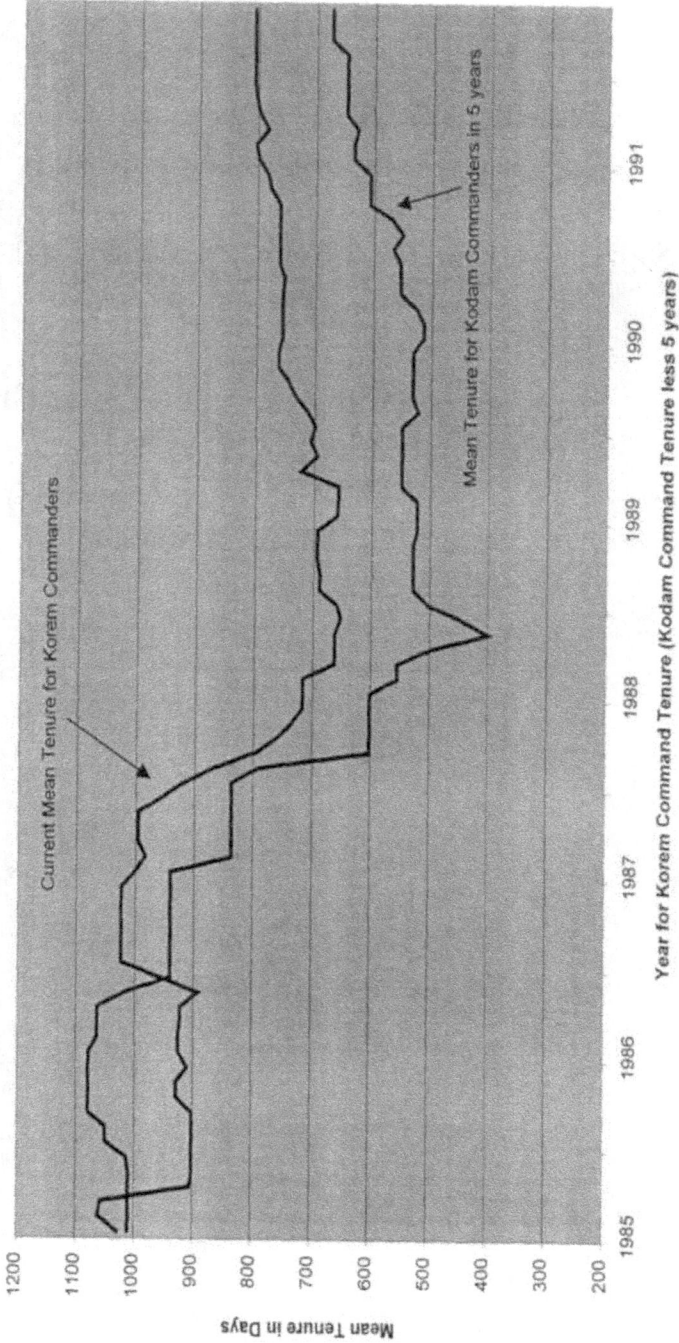

GOVERNORS OF THE NATIONAL MILITARY ACADEMY AND CADET INTAKE[1]

Entered Academy	Governor AMN/Akmil	Date Graduated	Class Number	Total Graduates
July 1957		June 1960	1	59
1958		June 1961	2	151
1959		June 1962	3	112
1960		June 1963	4	113
1961		June 1964	5	280
1962		June 1965	6	433
1963	Soerono	June 1966	7	243
1964		June 1967	8	203
1965		June 1968	9	465
1966		Dec. 1970	10	437
1967	Tahir	Dec. 1971	11	329
1968		Dec. 1972	12	389
Jan. 1970	Solichin	Dec. 1973	13	436
1971		Dec. 1974	14	434

---

1 Note: no data are available on the total numbers of cadets admitted to the academy.

1972	Sarwo Edie	Dec. 1975	15	304
1973		Dec. 1976	16	85
1974		Dec. 1977	17	79
1975		Dec. 1978	18	93
1976	Wiyogo	Dec. 1980	19	102
1977		Mar. 1981	20	146
1978		Mar. 1982	21	85
Aug. 1979	Wibisono	Mar. 1983	22	184
1980		Mar. 1984	23	244

AGE AT TIME OF APPOINTMENT TO COMMAND POSTS

The ballooning size of the officer corps coupled with the frequency with which classmates succeeded one another in command positions has further exacerbated the structural problems within the Army by increasing the age at which officers are appointed to each rung on the career ladder. Here, we find a direct and obvious correlation: as the promotional logjam intensified, officers had to wait longer before being appointed to command positions. As a consequence, these officers were older than their predecessors at the time of appointment.

The data illustrate this relationship in no uncertain terms. During the 1990s, the mean age at time of appointment at each command level increased by two to three years. The mean age at which officers were appointed as Kodim commanders increased from 40.5 years in 1989-1990 to a high of forty-three years in 1995-1996. The mean age at time of appointment for Korem commanders rose from forty-four years in 1987-1989 to forty-six years during the 1991-1997 period.[1] And the age of Kodam commanders rose from a mean of forty-eight years in the late 1980s to fifty to fifty-one years during the 1992-1997 period.[2] In an effort to offset this development, the tenure of these officers was reduced; this, however, could only provide a partial remedy to the problem.

These findings have two major implications for the original model

---

[1] Without information on the date of birth for the large number of officers involved, we have calculated these figures based on an average age of 22 at time of graduation plus the number of years between time of graduation and time of appointment to the given command.

[2] These figures were calculated based on the actual date of birth for 86 out of 90 officers who were appointed as Kodam commanders during the 1985-1998 period.

presented in chapter one. First, even with the significant decrease in mean tenure, an increase in age at time of appointment meant an increase in the age of officers at the time they vacate their command posts. This increase in the age at which officers vacate a position is an indication of the pressure of excessive numbers of officers; a fall in the age at which officers leave a post signals a decrease in this pressure. Second, the greater the age of an officer at the time he vacates a post, the less likely it is that he will be appointed to a higher post on the career ladder. In other words, there is an inverse relationship between the age at which officers complete their tours of duty and career prospects. These findings allow us further to refine our original model. The decline in command tenure was not a simple result of the increase in the size of classes graduating from the AMN. Rather, increased class size and the practice of allowing outgoing officers to recommend their replacements led to increased age of officers both entering and vacating posts. This development provided yet another reason why the military needed to reduce command tenure.

Finally, it is essential to note that in 1997-1998 the mean age at which officers are appointed as Kodim commanders decreased sharply. This clearly reflects the much smaller size of the classes that graduated from Akmil during the late 1970s and early 1980s, the members of which are now reaching middle ranks and filling Kodim and Korem commands. This phenomenon is first appearing at the Kodim level, but we can say with confidence that in the near future a similar decrease will appear at the Korem and later the Kodam levels as well.

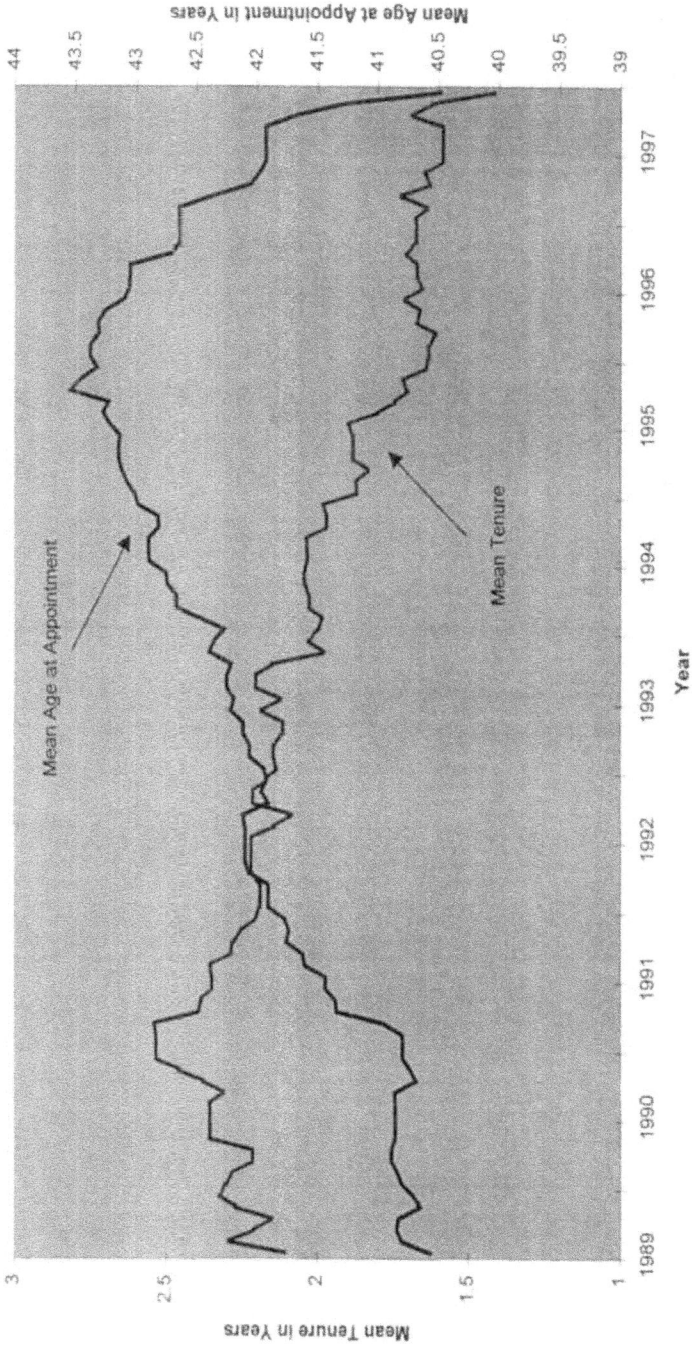

Figure A2.1a: Mean Tenure and Age at Time of Appointment for Kodim Commanders (1985-1997)

Figure A2.1b: Mean Tenure and Age at Time of Appointment for Kodam Commanders
(1985-1998)

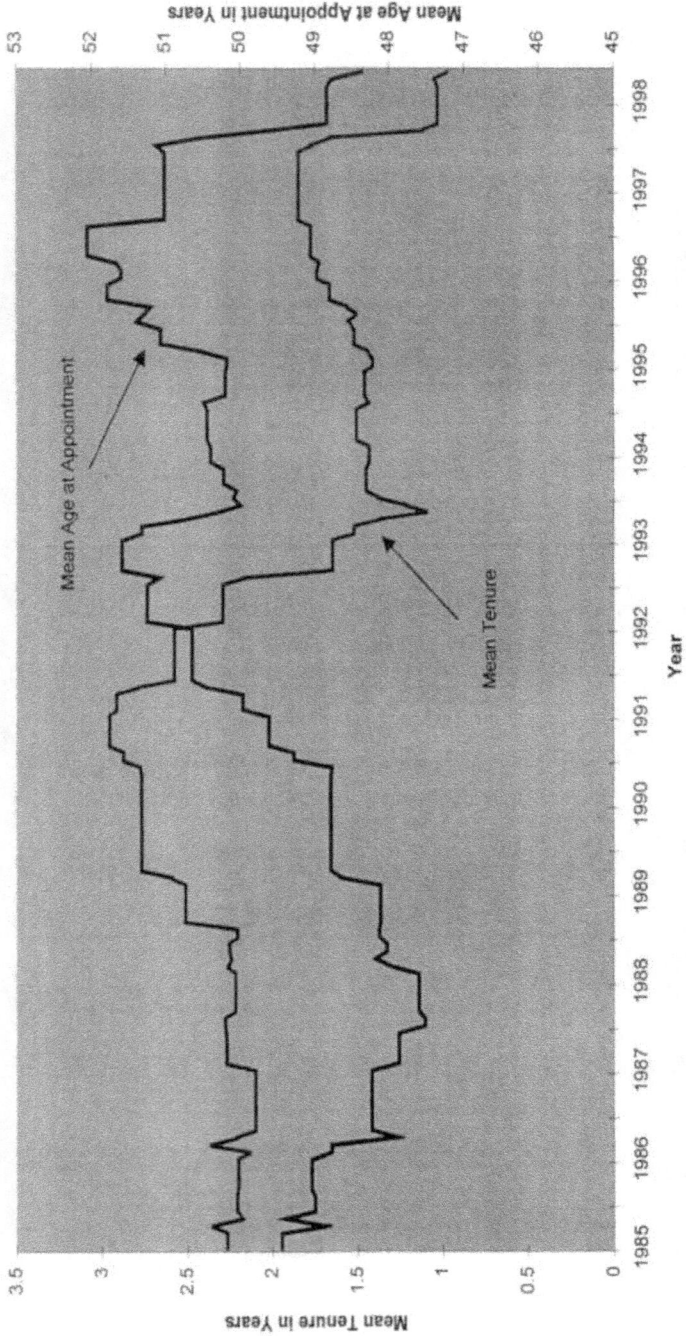

BIBLIOGRAPHY

"Analisis Perkembangan Sosial-Politik Menjelang Pemilu 1997 dan SU-MPR 1998," posted on <APAKABAR@clark.net>.

Anderson, Ben. "Current Data on the Indonesian Military Elite." *Indonesia* 40 (October 1985).

_____. "Current Data on the Indonesian Military Elite." *Indonesia* 48 (October 1989).

Anderson, B. R. O'G, and Ruth McVey. *A Preliminary Analysis of the October 1, 1965 Coup in Indonesia*. Ithaca: Modern Indonesia Project, 1971.

Britton, Peter. "Military Professionalism in Indonesia: Javanese and Western Military Traditions." PhD dissertation, Monash University, 1982.

Callahan, Mary. "The Origins of Military Rule in Burma." PhD dissertation, Cornell University, 1996.

Chua Beng Huat. "Looking for Democratization in Post-Soeharto Indonesia." *Contemporary Southeast Asia* 15,2 (September 1993).

Crouch, Harold. *The Army and Politics in Indonesia*. Ithaca: Cornell University Press, 1988.

Daftar Alumni Akademi Militer 1948-1996

Departemen Pertahanan Keamanan. *Tanya-Jawab Dwi Fungsi dan Kekaryaan ABRI*. Jakarta: Ssospol Hankam, 1979.

_____. *Dwi Fungsi dan Kekaryaan ABRI*. Jakarta: Ssospol Hankam, 1979.

Editors. "Current Data on the Indonesian Military Elite: July 1, 1989 to January 1, 1992." *Indonesia* 53 (April 1992).

_____. "Current Data on the Indonesian Military Elite: January 1, 1992-April 3, 1993." *Indonesia* 55 (April 1993).

_____. "Current Data on the Indonesian Military Elite: January 1, 1992 to August 31, 1993." *Indonesia* 56 (October 1993).

_____. "Current Data on the Indonesian Military Elite: September 1, 1993 to August 31, 1994." *Indonesia* 58 (October 1994).

_____. "Current Data on the Indonesian Military Elite: September 1, 1993 to September 30, 1995." *Indonesia* 60 (October 1995).

_____. "Structural Constraints on the Indonesian Military in the mid-1990s." *Indonesia*. 63 (April 1997).

Feisal Tanjung. *ABRI-Islam Mitra Sejati*. Jakarta: Sinar Harapan, 1997.

Indria Samego, ed., *Peran Sospol ABRI: Masalah dan Prospeknya*. (unpublished report, Pusat Penelitian dan Pengembangan Politik dan Kewilayahan-LIPI, 1997).

Istiqlal. "Analisis CPDS," obtained from: owner-indonesia-l@indopubs.com.

Jenkins, David. *Suharto and his Generals: Indonesian Military Politics 1975-1983*. Ithaca: Cornell Modern Indonesia Project, 1984.

Liddle, R. William. "Indonesia's Threefold Crisis." *Journal of Democracy* 3,4 (October 1992).

Lowry, Robert. *The Armed Forces of Indonesia*. St. Leonards: Allen & Unwin, 1996.

Luckham, Robin. *The Nigerian Military: A Sociological Analysis of Authority and Revolt, 1960-1967*. Cambridge: Cambridge University Press, 1971.

Mako, Akabri. *Sejarah Akademi Angkatan Bersenjata RI (1945-1971)*. 2 vols. (1993).

Malley, Michael. "Who is Running the Regions? Regional Political Leadership in Indonesia, 1966-1996." Paper presented at the 49th Annual Meeting of the Association for Asian Studies, Chicago, March 13-16, 1997.

MacFarling, Ian. *The Dual Function of the Indonesian Armed Forces: Military Politics in Indonesia*. Sydney: Australian Defence Studies Centre, The University of New South Wales, 1996.

McVey, Ruth. "The Post-Revolutionary Transformation of the Indonesian Army." *Indonesia* 11 (April 1971), and No. 13 (April 1972).

Nugroho Notosusanto and Ismail Saleh. *The Coup Attempt of the 'September 30th Movement' in Indonesia*. Jakarta: Penbimbing, 1988.

Schwarz, Adam. *A Nation in Waiting: Indonesia in the 1990s*. Boulder:

Westview Press, 1994.

Singh, Bilveer. *The Dual Function of the Indonesian Armed Forces: Origins, Actualization, and Implementations for Stability and Development.* Singapore: Singapore Institute of International Affairs, 1995.

Stepan, Alfred. *The Military in Politics: Changing Patterns in Brazil.* Princeton: Princeton University Press, 1971.

Sundhaussen, Ulf. *The Road to Power.* Kuala Lumpur: Oxford University Press, 1982.

Tanter, Richard. 'Intelligence Agencies and Third World Militarization: A Case Study of Indonesia, 1966-1989." PhD dissertation, Monash University, 1991.

Whitten, Guy D., and Henry S. Bienen. "A Political Violence and Time in Power." *Armed Forces and Society* 23,2 (Winter 1966).

NEWSPAPERS AND MAGAZINES

Angkatan Bersenjata

Bernas

Forum Keadilan

Gatra

Jawa Pos

Kedaulatan Rakyat

Kompas

Media Indonesia

Merdeka

Mimbar Kekaryaan

Pikiran Rakyat

Republika

Sinar

Suara Merdeka

Suara Pembaruan

Surabaya Post

Surya

Sydney Morning Herald

Tempo

Tiras

Waspada

GLOSSARY

ABRI	Angkatan Bersenjata Republik Indonesia (Armed Forces Academy of the Republic of Indonesia)
Akabri	Akademi Angkatan Bersenjata Republik Indonesia (Academy of the Armed Forces of Indonesia)
Akmil Jurtek	Akademi Militer Jurusan Teknik (Military Technology Academy)
AMN	Akademi Militer Nasional (National Military Academy)
bupati	regent
dinas karya	non-military duty (in civil service or government)
DPR	Dewan Perwakilan Rakyat (People's Representative Council, Parliament)
dwifungsi	dual function. Doctrine stating that the armed forces have both a military and a socio-political role
Golkar	Golongan Karya (Functional Group, the ruling party)
Kabupaten	Regency (administrative unit)
kekaryaan	non-military duty (in civil service or government)
Kodam	Komando Daerah Militer (Regional Military Command)
Kodim	Komando Distrik Militer (District Military Command)
Kopassus	Komando Pasukan Khusus (Special Forces Command)
Koramil	Komando Rayon Militer (Sub-District Military Command)

Korem	Komando Resort Militer (Sub-Regional Military Command)
Kostrad	Komando Strategis Angkatan Darat (Army Strategic Command)
kyai	Muslim teacher or scholar
Lemhanas	Lembaga Pertahanan Nasional (National Defense Institute)
LIPI	Lembaga Ilmu Pengetahuan Indonesia (Indonesian Academy of Sciences)
Menko Polkam	Menteri Koordinator Politik dan Keamanan (Coordinating Minister for Politics and Security)
MPR	Majelis Permusyawaratan Rakyat (People's Consultative Assembly)
PDI	Partai Demokrat Indonesia (Indonesian Democratic Party)
Pepabri	Persatuan Purnawirawan ABRI (Association of Retired Members of the Armed Forces of the Republic of Indonesia)
PKI	Partai Komunis Indonesia (Indonesian Communist Party)
Secapa	Sekolah Calon Perwira (Officer Candidate School)
ulama	Muslim teacher or scholar
Walikota	mayor

www.ingramcontent.com/pod-product-compliance
Lightning Source LLC
Chambersburg PA
CBHW020357270326
41926CB00007B/473